Source SDK Game Development Essentials

Develop engaging and immersive mods with
Source SDK

Brett Bernier

PUBLISHING

BIRMINGHAM - MUMBAI

Source SDK Game Development Essentials

First published: February 2014

Production Reference: 1140214

Published by Packt Publishing Ltd.
Livery Place
35 Livery Street
Birmingham B3 2PB, UK.

ISBN 978-1-84969-592-3

www.packtpub.com

Cover Image by Suresh Mogre (suresh.mogre.99@gmail.com)

Credits

Author
Brett Bernier

Reviewers
Dennis Glowacki

Tim Kitevski

Kyle Langley

Kenny Sperling

Mike Taret

Acquisition Editors
Antony Lowe

Meeta Rajani

Content Development Editor
Madhuja Chaudhari

Technical Editors
Mario D'Souza

Venu Manthena

Shruti Rawool

Nachiket Vartak

Copy Editors
Brandt D'Mello

Mradula Hegde

Gladson Monteiro

Adithi Shetty

Project Coordinator
Kranti Berde

Proofreaders
Simran Bhogal

Maria Gould

Indexer
Mariammal Chettiyar

Production Coordinator
Aparna Bhagat

Cover Work
Aparna Bhagat

About the Author

Brett Bernier has been a creator since he could hold a LEGO brick and a gamer since he was old enough to hold a controller. After his father introduced him to First-Person Shooters, it didn't take long for him to want to create his own world. A lunch time discussion with Chris, his childhood friend and band mate, inspired him to take action and download Valve's Hammer 3.4 to create a Counter-Strike map. While looking for mapping tips online, he stumbled across a small, close-knit community of Half-Life mappers at The Whole Half-Life (TWHL). Brett, also known as Tetsu0, quickly honed his skills with the help of the community's tutorials and forums. When the Source SDK launched with Half-Life 2, he was hesitant to make the jump from GoldSource (Half-Life) to Source (Half-Life 2), but once made, he did not look back. He is currently employed as a Control System Technician at ETTER Engineering in Bristol, Connecticut, and is pursuing his Bachelor's Degree in Electronics Engineering Technology at the University of Hartford. He has been creating maps for the Half-Life game series since 2002.

I would like to thank my entire family for all their love and support; I love each and every one of you with all my heart. Court, thank you for the encouragement and free refills on those Sundays I spent writing at the coffee shop. I would like to thank the members and moderators of the Half-Life Mapping forum, twhl.info for creating a welcoming, supportive community. You all have been a fantastic source of inspiration, help, and support. Without you folks, this book would not have been possible.

I'd also like to thank the fine people at Valve Software for supporting the development community, and for granting permission to use their materials in this book.

Unfortunately, during the writing of this book, a close member of my family was taken away. I love and miss you Uncle Lou, this one is for you.

About the Reviewers

Dennis Glowacki is a 3D environment artist at Emotional Robots Inc. and an avid Source engine mod creator. He has released several projects including Strider Mountain, The Citizen 2, and Hypercube: Source. He recently worked on another book called *How to Become a Video Game Artist, Sam R. Kennedy, Watson-Guptil,* (ISBN: 978-0-8230-0809-4).

I'd like to thank Phillip from `PlanetPhillip.com` for being a good friend, especially during my Source engine development days and for continuing to support the Source engine modding community. Anyone interested in playing the best Source mods should check out his new website (`RunThinkShootLive.com`).

Tim Kitevski has for many years worked as a 3D artist within the video game industry. Having worked on various titles ranging from First-Person Shooters to Flight Simulators to Mining Equipment Training, his first steps within this field were with the first Half-Life and its main editing suite, back then known as WorldCraft. Since then he has had a keen interest in the ever-evolving Source engine produced by Valve software. He has spent many years using the Source SDK and its tools for both individual projects and group modding. In doing so, he gained a solid foundation of knowledge when developing the Source engine.

Kyle Langley is a self-taught game designer currently working for Emotional Robots Inc. He has also worked on Free Realms with Sony Online Entertainment and Transformers: Fall of Cybertron with High Moon Studios. He is the author of *Learn Programming With Unreal Script, CreateSpace Independent Publishing Platform,* which is aimed at teaching beginners the concepts of object-oriented programming as well as the beginning aspects of programming for the Unreal Development Kit. You can find more of his work at his website (`www.dotvawxgames.com`).

Kenny Sperling is an environmental designer with a passion for interaction and exploration. With experience in both conventional and contemporary design, he develops levels for games as well as real-world landscapes. His design process includes a strong understanding of how people interact with their environments, a drive to pursue sophisticated technical strategies, and a conviction to seek out atypical design solutions.

Kenny has designed several award-winning environmental concepts, and has consistently been active in community content development for numerous games, including Counter-Strike (CS:S/CS:GO).

Mike Taret is a passionate 3D artist currently residing in Chicago, USA; he also lived for about 13 years in France. Also known as "Az", he has been modding Source for seven years now, and is currently working on a mod called SourceForts 2 with several other people across the world. He considers himself a 3D generalist with his strongest skills focused around hard-surface modeling, texturing, and problem solving. He has worked with many software and engines such as Source SDK, UDK, Autodesk Maya, Autodesk 3ds Max, Photoshop, and a few others. You can find some of his work at www.az3d.net.

I'd like to thank my parents for supporting me, Felipe G. Silveira for being a great friend, and Matt Battaglia for pushing me to be what I am now.

www.PacktPub.com

Support files, eBooks, discount offers and more

You might want to visit www.PacktPub.com for support files and downloads related to your book.

Did you know that Packt offers eBook versions of every book published, with PDF and ePub files available? You can upgrade to the eBook version at www.PacktPub.com and as a print book customer, you are entitled to a discount on the eBook copy. Get in touch with us at service@packtpub.com for more details.

At www.PacktPub.com, you can also read a collection of free technical articles, sign up for a range of free newsletters and receive exclusive discounts and offers on Packt books and eBooks.

http://PacktLib.PacktPub.com

Do you need instant solutions to your IT questions? PacktLib is Packt's online digital book library. Here, you can access, read and search across Packt's entire library of books.

Why Subscribe?

- Fully searchable across every book published by Packt
- Copy and paste, print and bookmark content
- On demand and accessible via web browser

Free Access for Packt account holders

If you have an account with Packt at www.PacktPub.com, you can use this to access PacktLib today and view nine entirely free books. Simply use your login credentials for immediate access.

Table of Contents

Preface

Source SDK Development Essentials outlines the essential knowledge one needs to create maps and scripts for games using Valve's Source Engine. Valve, the videogame company behind Source, releases a Software Development Kit (SDK) with each game they produce. Counter-Strike: Source, Counter-Strike: Global Offensive, and Team Fortress 2 might be household names for some gamers, and the maps in those games were created with the Source SDK. Valve also released the Source SDK base for free in 2012, so anyone can download it and start creating for free.

This book is a walkthrough of the steps required to start producing professional environments and scripts. Because it's the same set of tools the professionals use, you can get the same professional results! This book is meant for gamers who want to get more out of their game, get their ideas down in 3D, and do it all without the need for any coding knowledge.

What this book covers

Chapter 1, Getting Started with the Source SDK, serves to get you situated with the tools and introduces you to Steam, the SDK, and Mod creation.

Chapter 2, Grasping Hammer, is where you will spend most of your development time. This chapter will introduce you to your new tools, and teach you how to navigate in 2D and 3D spaces.

Chapter 3, Shaping Your World, teaches you how to create and modify brushes while introducing you to some key terminology. The brush is the basic building block of any source level.

Chapter 4, Textures, Terrain, and Props, teaches you how to detail your world by adding textures to brushes, creating flowing terrain, and placing prop models.

Chapter 5, Importing Custom Content, teaches you how to create your own textures and import custom content. Lots of mods and maps have their own custom content.

Chapter 6, Lighting and Compiling, teaches you how to bring light to your creations. It also covers compiling concepts and error checking.

Chapter 7, Triggers and the Input/Output System, teaches you how to master this system. The Input/Output system is the heart and soul of Source's scripts.

Chapter 8, Trains and Camera Systems, brings life to stationary objects. It also teaches you how to use different types of cameras.

Chapter 9, NPC Movement Basics, teaches you what it takes to get Non-Playable Characters (NPCs) moving in this chapter. NPCs play a huge role in storytelling and immersion.

Chapter 10, Advanced NPC Scripting, teaches you how to create squads and control NPCs on a more macroscopic scale.

Chapter 11, Source Particle Editor, teaches you the ins and outs of Source's powerful particle editor. Particles play a key role making believable special effects.

What you need for this book

You will need Steam, a high speed internet connection, and just some time. In order to get the most out of this book, you'll want to purchase a copy of one of Valve's Half-Life 2 games, as this book focuses on scripts and development for *Half-Life 2: Episode Two*. It's not necessary to purchase a game; however, you can create a mod for free with the Source SDK and create your own game from scratch.

Who this book is for

If you are a gamer who wants to make your own games, levels, or mods, for any game using the Source engine, this book is ideal for you. You do not need to know any special programming languages in order to jump in and start creating!

Conventions

In this book, you will find a number of styles of text that distinguish between different kinds of information. Here are some examples of these styles, and an explanation of their meaning.

Code words in text, database table names, folder names, filenames, file extensions, pathnames, dummy URLs, user input, and Twitter handles are shown as follows: "The `mapsrc` folder is where all your maps should be saved."

A block of code is set as follows:

```
"LightmappedGeneric"
{
  "$basetexture" "mytextures/texture01"
  "$surfaceprop" "wood"
}
```

New terms and **important words** are shown in bold. Words that you see on the screen, in menus or dialog boxes for example, appear in the text like this: "click on the **Install Steam** button in the top-right corner of the web page".

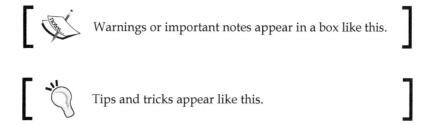

> Warnings or important notes appear in a box like this.

> Tips and tricks appear like this.

Reader feedback

Feedback from our readers is always welcome. Let us know what you think about this book—what you liked or may have disliked. Reader feedback is important for us to develop titles that you really get the most out of.

To send us general feedback, simply send an e-mail to feedback@packtpub.com, and mention the book title via the subject of your message.

If there is a topic that you have expertise in and you are interested in either writing or contributing to a book, see our author guide on www.packtpub.com/authors.

Customer support

Now that you are the proud owner of a Packt book, we have a number of things to help you to get the most from your purchase.

Downloading the example code

You can download the example code files for all Packt books you have purchased from your account at http://www.packtpub.com. If you purchased this book elsewhere, you can visit http://www.packtpub.com/support and register to have the files e-mailed directly to you.

Downloading the color images of this book

We also provide you a PDF file that has color images of the screenshots/diagrams used in this book. The color images will help you better understand the changes in the output. You can download this file from: http://www.packtpub.com/sites/default/files/downloads/5923OT_ColoredImages.pdf.

Errata

Although we have taken every care to ensure the accuracy of our content, mistakes do happen. If you find a mistake in one of our books—maybe a mistake in the text or the code—we would be grateful if you would report this to us. By doing so, you can save other readers from frustration and help us improve subsequent versions of this book. If you find any errata, please report them by visiting http://www.packtpub.com/submit-errata, selecting your book, clicking on the **errata submission form** link, and entering the details of your errata. Once your errata are verified, your submission will be accepted and the errata will be uploaded on our website, or added to any list of existing errata, under the Errata section of that title. Any existing errata can be viewed by selecting your title from http://www.packtpub.com/support.

Piracy

Piracy of copyright material on the Internet is an ongoing problem across all media. At Packt, we take the protection of our copyright and licenses very seriously. If you come across any illegal copies of our works, in any form, on the Internet, please provide us with the location address or website name immediately so that we can pursue a remedy.

Please contact us at copyright@packtpub.com with a link to the suspected pirated material.

We appreciate your help in protecting our authors, and our ability to bring you valuable content.

Questions

You can contact us at questions@packtpub.com if you are having a problem with any aspect of the book, and we will do our best to address it.

Getting Started with
the Source SDK

1

The **Source SDK** is a collection of software used to create custom content for games made with Valve's Source engine. Also known as authoring tools, the Source SDK contains all the tools you need to start creating your own levels. In order to get started with the Source SDK, you first need to get a hold of **Steam**. Steam is Valve's entertainment platform that allows its users to download and play a multitude of different games.

In this chapter, we will cover the following topics:

- Downloading and installing Steam
- Gaining access to the SDK
- Glancing at the tools
- Creating your own modification (mod) with the Source SDK

So, let's get started!

Installing Steam

You might ask yourself what is Steam, and why do I need it? First and foremost, the only way to gain access to the Source SDK is by downloading the SDK or a Valve game that uses the Source engine. All of Valve's Source engine games are downloaded and managed with a program called Steam. Steam lets you purchase, organize, and update thousands of games, and it's completely free.

In order to download and install Steam, you need to visit `store.steampowered.com`, and click on the **Install Steam** button in the top-right corner of the web page, as shown in the following screenshot:

This will redirect you to another page where you can download the actual installation file. After you have downloaded and installed Steam, you need to log in or create a new user account if you do not already have one. All you need is a valid e-mail address in order to create a new Steam account.

Getting your tools

Great! You have installed Steam. Now what? There are a multitude of games that run on the Source engine. There are also many different versions of the Source engine: 2006, 2007, 2013, and multiplayer and single player variants for each. This book will focus on *Half-Life 2: Episode Two* (HL2: EP2) since it's the most recent single player build of the Source engine at the time of writing this book. In order to create content for HL2: EP2, you just need to own a copy of the game. Steam makes it easy to install games. So, if you haven't already, purchase and install HL2: EP2.

 You don't need HL2: EP2 to follow this book. The principles taught cover the Source SDK tools, which are applicable to multiple games.

Instructions for installing Half-Life 2: Episode Two

Downloading and installing games with Steam is easy! Steam lets you securely purchase any game and will automatically install them once downloaded. The steps for installing *Half-Life 2: Episode Two* are as follows:

1. Open Steam and log in.
2. In Steam, just below the main toolbar, you will see **STORE, LIBRARY, COMMUNITY**, and your username in a large white font. Click on **STORE**.

3. Search for `Half-Life 2: Episode Two`, purchase it, and install it.

4. You can monitor the download progress within the **Downloads** tab in the **LIBRARY** drop-down menu. HL2: EP2 will begin to install automatically once the download is complete.

The **STORE** is located in the top-left corner of Steam as shown in the following screenshot:

Browse for `Half-Life 2: Episode Two` as shown in the following screenshot. You can also get any other Source game.

Once the download and install is complete, launch the game and play around with the engine you will be developing for, as shown in the following screenshot:

The Source SDK tools overview

All the SDK tools come with the game, so you don't need to install anything extra. (This also means you don't need to wait for something else to download!) The tools are located in the `Steam\steamapps\common\Half-Life 2\bin` folder. The folder is packed with applications, batch files, and DLLs, but there are a few key programs that we're interested in right now. In the `bin` folder, you will see **Hammer**, **HLMV**, and **HLFacePoser**. Hammer Editor is the tool you will most likely use; it is the application that you use to actually create the levels (maps). HLMV or Half-Life Model Viewer is a tool you can use to inspect game models in detail. HLFacePoser is used to sync lips to speech, and create custom scenes and NPC interactions.

[At the time of writing this book, FacePoser is broken—this will not be covered.]

The Source SDK

Half-Life 2: Episode Two ships with its own set of authoring tools, but if you want to make your own mod, you need the Source SDK. The Source SDK is a program that organizes all the authoring tools for specific mods and engine builds and has the ability to automatically create a mod based on the code from *Half-Life 2: Episode Two*. If you want to create your own mod, you will need to grab the Source SDK.

Installing the Source SDK

Installing the Source SDK is just as easy as any regular game. The best part is its price: free! The steps for installing the Source SDK are as follows:

1. In the top-left corner of the games library, select the dropdown that says **All Games** and select **Tools**.

2. Find the **Source SDK** in the list of **Tools**.

3. Right-click on **Source SDK** and select **Install game**, or just double-click to begin the download process.

4. You can monitor the download progress within the **Downloads** tab in the **LIBRARY**. The **Source SDK** will begin to install automatically once the download is complete.

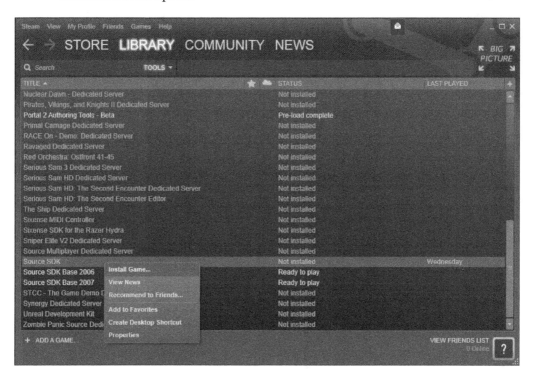

The Source SDK overview

When you first launch the Source SDK, it will need a minute or so to copy files and complete the install, but once that is complete, you're ready to go! You will notice that the Source SDK contains a variety of tools, documents, and links. At the very bottom are two fields labeled **Engine Version** and **Current Game**. **Engine Version** is used to select which version of the Source engine you would like to develop for.

The later engine versions have more features and graphics upgrades compared to the earlier versions. There is also the **Source Engine MP** option, which lets you create maps for Valve's multiplayer games such as *Counter-Strike: Source* and *Team Fortress 2*.

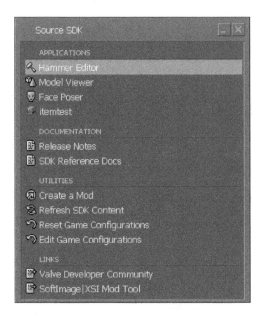

Applications

In the **APPLICATIONS** list, you will see **Hammer Editor**, **Model Viewer**, **Face Poser**, and **itemtest**. Hey, doesn't this look like the set of authoring tools we had for HL2: EP2? It is, with the exception of **itemtest** that allows you to look into details about specific games items such as the items available in *Team Fortress 2*.

Documentation

In the **DOCUMENTATION** list, you will see **Release Notes** and **SDK Reference Docs**. The **Release Notes** option will link you to the **Valve Developer Community** website that describes the changes made to the current version of the Source SDK. **SDK Reference Docs** will link you to the **Valve Developer Community** website's collection of notes about every aspect of the Source SDK.

Utilities

In the **UTILITIES** list, you will see **Create a Mod, Refresh SDK Content, Reset Game Configurations**, and **Edit Game Configurations**. **Create a Mod** will open a wizard that allows you to create your own modification, or mod, for a certain Source game. **Refresh SDK Content** will refresh all the game content in the event that the Source SDK is not functioning properly. **Reset Game Configurations** will return all games to their default configurations. **Edit Game Configurations** will allow you to modify the path of any game you want.

Links

In the **LINKS** list, you will see **Valve Developer Community** and **Softimage|XSI Mod Tool**. **Valve Developer Community** will link you to the main page of **Valve Developer Community**. **Softimage|XSI Mod Tool** will link you to an Autodesk website where you can download a free version of character modeling and animation software that is compatible with the Source engine.

Creating your own modification (mod)

So you have this amazing idea for a video game and want to create your own mod. You want to include lasers and Samurai, and you want to make a fast-paced, WWII-era, team-based shoot-em-up game called *Samurai Laser Paratroopers*. Well, guess what—the Source engine can do this, and the Source SDK makes the mod setup easy! In this example, we will be creating a multiplayer Mod for the 2007 Source engine from a template:

1. To create your very own Half-Life 2 mod, double-click on the **Create a Mod** utility.

2. Select the **Start a Multiplayer mod from a Template** radio button on the first prompt of the **Create a Mod** wizard and then click on **Next**.

3. In the first entry, specify the drive directory location where you want your game to be stored. I chose `C:\SLP\` for easy access. In the second entry, specify the name of the mod you want to create, and click on **Next** to continue.

4. Choose the options you want available in your mod.

5. The wizard will then copy all the necessary files into the directory you have specified.

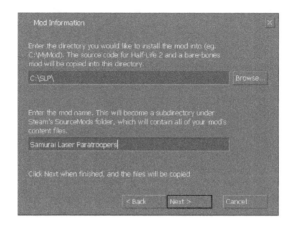

The instructions are pretty straightforward. Choose carefully when you select the options shown in the following screenshot; they're harder to change later on:

Have patience, we're almost done!

Now, let's take a look at the folders the wizard has created. There are four folders in your new mod's folder (shown here as `C:\SLP`). Three of those folders have suffixes of "src" as shown in the following screenshot:

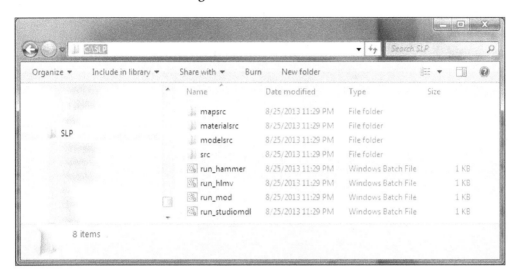

The `mapsrc` folder is where all your maps should be saved (although you can always save your maps elsewhere). All texture and material files go into the `materialsrc` folder, while all models should be saved in the `modelsrc` folder. The code generated specifically for your mod is saved in the `src` folder. Utilizing these folders to store all your source materials will make your life easier later on.

Restart Steam and check out your library of games. Your new mod is in there!

Also take a look at the Source SDK; your mod will be listed as one of the games in the engine build you selected, as shown in the following screenshot:

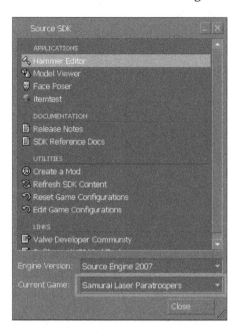

When you create a mod with the Source SDK wizard, it creates a barebones game. You will need to dive into the game code to make your mod what you want it to be. This book does not cover custom code, but it's still relevant for mapping techniques for your custom mod.

Summary

Getting your hands on Steam is quick and easy. It is required to use the Source SDK tools, and it is also useful for keeping your games and tools organized. Once Steam is installed, downloading and installing *Half-Life 2: Episode Two* is a snap. Creating a mod is a great way to begin developing your own game with the source engine base code, but you still need to code to get what you want out of the game. Let's pick up the Hammer and see what we can do!

2
Grasping Hammer

Now that you have everything installed, I bet you're itching to start creating! We're not there yet because there are still some things to cover. This chapter serves to shed some light on the mysteries of mapping.

In this chapter, we will cover the following topics:

- Learning some basic terminology
- Opening **Hammer** for the first time
- Navigating the 2D and 3D viewports
- Customizing your user interface
- Developing some basic organizational skills

Let us begin.

Terminology

In this book, I will be guiding you through many examples using Hammer. There are a handful of terms that will recur many times that you will need to know. It might be a good idea to bookmark this page, so you can flip back and refresh your memory.

Brush

A **brush** is a piece of world geometry created with block tool. Brushes make up the basic building blocks of a map and must be convex. A convex object's faces cannot see each other, while a concave object's faces can. Imagine if you're lying on the pitched roof of a generic house. You wouldn't be able to see the other side of the roof because the profile of the house is a convex pentagon. If you moved the point of the roof down inside the house, you would be able to see the other side of the roof because the profile would then be concave.

This can be seen in the following screenshot:

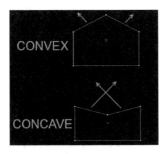

Got it? Good. Don't think you're limited by this; you can always create convex shapes out of more than one brush.

Since we're talking about houses, brushes are used to create the walls, floor, ceiling, and roof. Brushes are usually geometrically very simple; upon creation, common brushes have six faces and eight vertices like a cube.

The brushes are outlined in the following screenshot:

Not all brushes have six sides; however, the more advanced brushwork techniques can create brushes that have (almost) as many sides as you want. You need to be careful while making complex brushes with the more advanced tools though. This is because it can be quite easy to make an invalid solid if you're not careful.

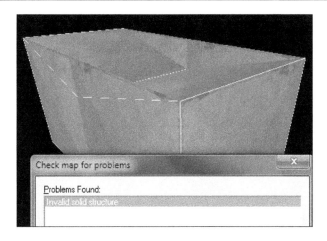

An invalid solid will cause errors during compilation and will make your map unplayable. A concave brush is an example of an invalid solid. World brushes are completely static or unmoving. If you want your brushes to have a special function, they need to be turned into entities.

Entity

An **entity** is anything in the game that has a special function. Entities come in two flavors: brush-based and point-based. A brush-based entity, as you can probably guess, is created from a brush. A sliding door or a platform lift are examples of brush-based entities. Point-based entities, on the other hand, are created in a point in space with the entity tool. Lights, models, sounds, and script events are all point-based entities. In the following figure, the models or props are highlighted:

World

The **world** is everything inside of a map that you create. Brushes, lights, triggers, sounds, models, and so on are all part of the world. They must all be contained within a sealed map made out of world brushes.

 A map must be completely sealed, but don't just enclose the whole thing in a hollow box. Putting your map in a box will increase the compile time and lower game performance because you're rendering a whole lot of faces you don't need to.

Void

The **void** is nothing or everything that isn't the world. The world must be sealed off from the void in order to function correctly when compiled and played in game. Imagine the void as outer space or a vacuum. World brushes seal off the world from the void. If there are any gaps in world brushes (or if there are any entities floating in the void), this will create a leak, and the engine will not be able to discern what the world is and what the void is. If a leak exists in your map, the engine will not know what is supposed to be seen during the compile! The map will compile, but performance-reducing side effects such as bland lighting and excess rendered polygons will plague your map.

Settings

If at any point in your mapping experience, Hammer doesn't seem to be operating the way you want it to be, go to **Tools | Options**, and see if there's any preferences you would like to change. You can customize general settings or options related to the 2D and 3D views. If you're coming from another editor, perhaps there's a setting that will make your Hammer experience similar to what you're used to.

Loading Hammer for the first time

You'll be opening `Steam\steamapps\common\Half-Life 2\bin` often, so you may want to create a desktop shortcut for easier access. Run `Hammer.bat` from the `bin` folder to launch **Valve Hammer Editor**, Valve's map (level) creator, so you can start creating a map. Hammer will prompt you to choose a game configuration, so choose which game you want to map for.

I will be using **Half-Life 2: Episode Two** in the following examples:

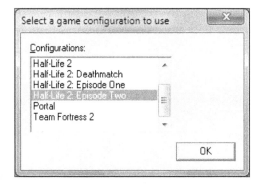

When you first open up Hammer, you will see a blank gray screen surrounded by a handful of menus, as shown in the following screenshot:

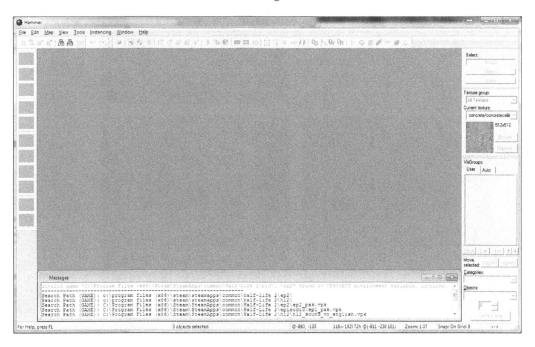

Like every other Microsoft Windows application, there is a main menu in the top-left corner of the screen that lets you open, save, or create a document. As far as Hammer is concerned, our documents are maps, and they are saved with the .vmf file extension. So let's open the **File** menu and load an example map so we can poke around a bit. Load the map titled Chapter2_Example.vmf.

The Hammer overview

In this section, we will be learning to recognize the different areas of Hammer and what they do. Being familiar with your environment is important!

Viewports

There are four main windows or viewports in Hammer, as shown in the following screenshot:

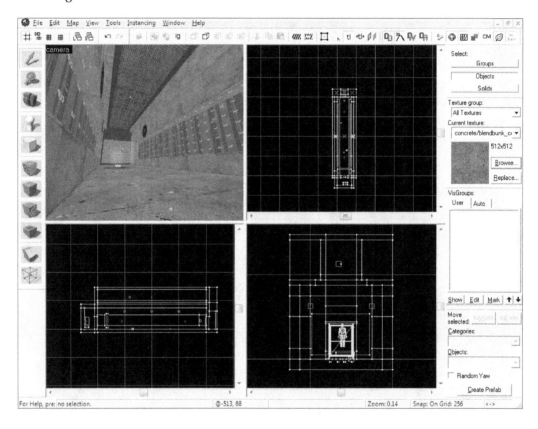

By default, the top-left window is the 3D view or **camera** view. The top-right window is the **top (x/y)** view, the bottom-right window is the **side (x/z)** view, and the bottom-left window is the **front (y/z)** view. If you would like to change the layout of the windows, simply click on the top-left corner of any window to change what is displayed.

In this book, I will be keeping the default layout but that does not mean you have to! Set up Hammer any way you'd like. For instance, if you would prefer your 3D view to be larger, grab the cross at the middle of the four screens and drag to extend the areas.

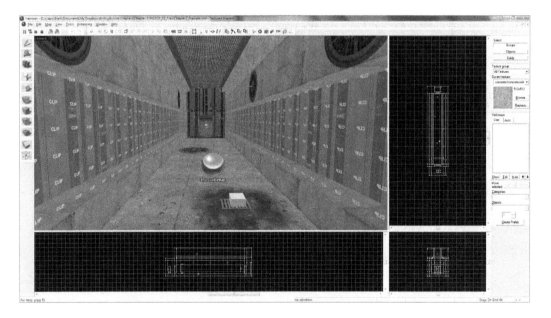

The 3D window has a few special 3D display types such as **Ray-Traced Preview** and **Lightmap Grid**. We will be learning more about these later, but for now, just know that **3D Ray-traced Preview** simulates the way light is cast. It does not mimic what you would actually see in-game, but it can be a good first step before compile to see what your lighting may look like.

The **3D Lighting Preview** will open in a new window and will update every time a camera is moved or a light entity is changed. You cannot navigate directly in the lighting preview window, so you will need to use the 2D cameras to change the viewing perspective.

 Some of the options might not be functional on certain Source engine builds.

The Map toolbar

Located to the left of the screen, the Map toolbar holds all the mapping tools. You will probably use this toolbar the most. The tools will each be covered in depth later on, but here's a basic overview, as shown in the following screenshot, starting from the first tool:

The Selection Tool

The Selection Tool is pretty self-explanatory; use this tool to select objects. The hot key for this is *Shift + S*. This is the tool that you will probably use the most. This tool selects objects in the 3D and 2D views and also lets you drag selection boxes in the 2D views.

The Magnify Tool

The Magnify Tool will zoom in and out in any view. You could also just use the mouse wheel if you have one or the + and – keys on the numerical keypad for the 2D views. The hot key for the magnify tool is *Shift + G*.

The Camera Tool

The Camera Tool enables 3D view navigation and lets you place multiple different cameras into the 2D views. Its hot key is *Shift + C*.

The Entity Tool

The Entity Tool places entities into the map. If clicked on the 3D view, an entity is placed on the closest brush to the mouse cursor. If used in the 2D view, a crosshair will appear noting the origin of the entity, and the *Enter* key will add it to the map at the origin. The entity placed in the map is specified by the object bar. The hot key is *Shift + E*.

The Block Tool

The Block Tool creates brushes. Drag a box in any 2D view and hit the *Enter* key to create a brush within the bounds of the box. The object bar specifies which type of brush will be created. The default is box and the hot key for this is *Shift + B*.

The Texture Tool

The Texture Tool allows complete control over how you paint your brushes. For now, just know where it is and what it does; the hot key is *Shift + A*.

The Apply Current Texture Tool

Clicking on the Apply Current Texture icon will apply the selected texture to the selected brush or brushes.

The Decal Tool

The Decal Tool applies decals and little detail textures to brushes and the hot key is *Shift + D*.

The Overlay Tool

The Overlay Tool is similar to the decal tool. However, overlays are a bit more powerful than decals. *Shift + O* will be the hot key.

The Clipping Tool

The Clipping Tool lets you slice brushes into two or more pieces, and the hot key is *Shift + X*.

The Vertex manipulation Tool

The Vertex manipulation Tool, or VM tool, allows you to move the individual vertices and edges of brushes any way you like. This is one of the most powerful tools you have in your toolkit! Using this tool improperly, however, is the easiest way to corrupt your map and ruin your day. Not to worry though, we'll learn about this in great detail later on. The hot key is *Shift + V*.

The selection mode bar

The selection mode bar (located at the top-right corner by default) lets you choose what you want to select. If **Groups** is selected, you will select an entire group of objects (if they were previously grouped) when you click on something. The **Objects** selection mode will only select individual objects within groups. **Solids** will only select solid objects.

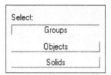

The texture bar

Located just beneath the selection mode toolbar, the texture bar, as shown, in the following screenshot, shows a thumbnail preview of your currently selected (active) texture and has two buttons that let you select or replace a texture. What a nifty tool, eh?

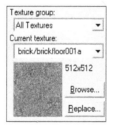

The filter control bar

The filter control bar controls your **VisGroups** (short for visual groups). **VisGroups** separate your map objects into different categories, similar to layers in the image editing software.

To make your mapping life a bit easier, you can toggle visibility of object groups. If, for example, you're trying to sculpt some terrain but keep getting your view blocked by tree models, you can just uncheck the **Props** box, as shown in the following screenshot, to hide all the trees!

There are multiple automatically generated **VisGroups** such as entities, displacements, and nodraws that you can easily filter through. Don't think you're limited to this though; you can create your own VisGroup with any selection at any time.

The object bar

The object bar lets you control what type of brush you are creating with the brush tool. This is also where you turn brushes into brush-based entities and create and place prefabs, as shown in the following screenshot:

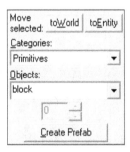

Navigating in 3D

You will be spending most of your time in the main four windows, so now let's get comfortable navigating in them, starting with the 3D viewport.

Looking around

Select the camera tool on the map tools bar. It's the third one down on the list and looks like a red 35 mm camera.

Holding the left mouse button while in the 3D view will allow you to look around from a stationary point. Holding the right mouse button will allow you to pan left, right, up, and down in the 3D space. Holding both left and right mouse buttons down together will allow you to move forward and backwards as well as pan left and right. Scrolling the mouse wheel will move the camera forward and backwards.

Practice flying down the example map hallway. While looking down the hallway, hold the right mouse button to rise up through the grate and see the top of the map.

If you would prefer another method of navigating in 3D, you can use the *W*, *S*, *A*, and *D* keys to move around while the left mouse button is pressed. Just like your normal FPS game, *W* moves forward in the direction of the camera, *S* moves backwards, and *A* and *D* move left and right, respectively. You can also move the mouse to look around while moving.

Being comfortable with the 3D view is necessary in order to become proficient in creating and scripting 3D environments. As with everything, practice makes perfect, so don't be discouraged if you find yourself hitting the wrong buttons.

Having the camera tool selected is not necessary to navigate in 3D. With any tool selected, hold Space bar while the cursor is in the 3D window to activate the 3D navigation mode. While holding Space bar, the navigation functions exactly as it does as if the camera tool was selected. Releasing Space bar will restore normal functionality to the currently selected tool. This can be a huge time saver down the line when you're working on very technical object placements.

Multiple cameras

If you find yourself bouncing around between different areas of the map, or even changing angles near the same object, you can create multiple cameras and juggle between them. With the camera tool selected, hold *Shift* and drag a line with the left mouse button in any 2D viewport. The start of the line will be the camera origin, and the end of the line will be the camera's target.

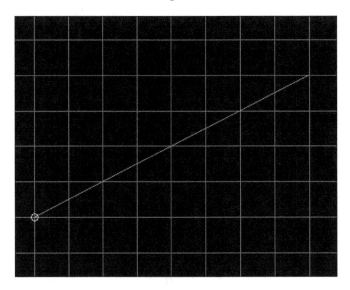

Whenever you create a new camera, the newly created camera becomes active and displays its view in the 3D viewport. To cycle between cameras, press the *Page Up* and *Page Down* buttons, or click on a camera in any 2D view. Camera locations are stored in the map file when you save, so you don't have to worry about losing them when you exit. Pressing the *Delete* key with a camera selected will remove the active camera. If you delete the only camera, your view will snap to the origin (0, 0, 0) but you will still be able to look around and create other cameras. In essence, you will always have at least one camera in your map.

Selecting objects in the 3D viewport

To select an object in the 3D viewport, you must have the selection tool active, as shown in the following screenshot. A quick way to activate the selection tool is to hit the *Esc* key while any tool is selected, or use the *Shift + S* hot key.

A selected brush or a group of brushes will be highlighted in red with yellow edges as shown in the following screenshot:

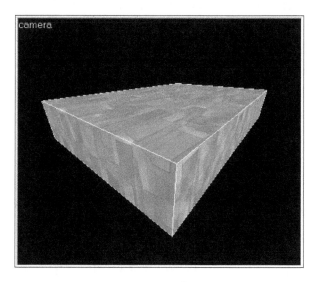

To deselect anything within the 3D window, click on any other brush, or on the background (void), or simply hit the *Esc* key. If you want to select an object behind another object, press and hold the left mouse button on the front object. This will cycle through all the objects that are located behind the cursor. You will be able to see the selected objects changing in the 2D and 3D windows about once per second. Simply release the mouse button to complete your selection.

To select multiple brushes or objects in the 3D window, hold *Ctrl* and left-click on multiple brushes. Clicking on a selected object while *Ctrl* is held will deselect the object. If you've made a mistake choosing objects, you can undo your selections with *Ctrl* + *Z* or navigate to **Edit | Undo**.

Navigating in 2D

Navigating in 2D is a bit different than 3D. Each 2D window has scroll bars like any webpage or text document, but there are some tips and tricks that can streamline the process.

Moving around

You can zoom in a 2D view by scrolling up the scroll wheel. Scrolling the scroll wheel down will zoom out. If you do not have a scroll wheel on your mouse, the magnify tool will be your best friend.

The magnify tool works just how you would expect it to: left-click to zoom in and right-click to zoom out.

 The + and – buttons on the keypad will also zoom in and out in 2D views if your cursor is inside one of them.

The minimum zoom (all the way out) is **0.01**. The maximum zoom (all the way in) is **256**. The current zoom amount is indicated in the bottom-right corner of the status bar, as shown in the following screenshot:

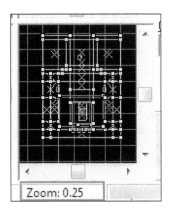

Panning the view is as easy as holding the Space bar and dragging the screen around with the left mouse button. You can also pan the view by using the up, down, left, and right arrows on the keyboard or using the scroll bars located to the right and bottom of each window.

Selecting objects in 2D

Just like the 3D view, selecting a brush in 2D is as easy as left-clicking on the center **X**, or one of the brush's edges. A selected object in the 2D view will be highlighted in red and have a yellow dashed line as a bounding box.

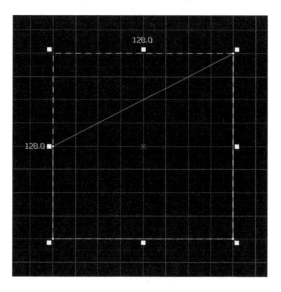

Just like the 3D view, multiple objects can be selected by holding *Ctrl* and left-clicking every object you want to select. Thankfully, the 2D view does not fall to the same selection pitfall as the 3D window, and clicking the void with *Ctrl* pressed will not deselect everything! Another way to select an object is to drag a selection box around it. Left-click and drag a selection box around the brush. Make sure the selection box surrounds the brush in at least two 2D views, and then hit *Enter* to select everything inside of that box. Objects that intersect with the box area will also be selected.

The bounding box you draw while clicking and dragging will follow the grid resolution. To get a more accurate bounding box for selecting objects, try decreasing the grid size with *[*, or hold *Alt* to ignore the grid completely.

The grid

The grid helps keep your brushes organized, and by default, objects snap to it—meaning one or more edges will forced to be aligned to it. The grid size is based on powers of 2 (1, 2, 4, 8, 16, 32, and so on), and ranges from 1 to 512. The main gridlines are white, while the origin of the map (the 0, 0, 0 point) is highlighted in green, and every 1024 units is highlighted in red. The default grid size is 64 units, but you may change this any time. To increase the grid size, press the] key. To decrease the grid size, press the [button. The size of the grid is indicated in the status bar at the bottom-right corner of the screen. Working with a grid will ensure that objects touch each other. If you're making the map boundaries without a grid and two objects aren't touching, you could easily create a leak.

It's good practice to stay with a grid size of 4, 8, or 16 for most of your level development. Only small details should be created with smaller grid sizes; once you're done, return to a larger grid size.

VisGroups

A VisGroup is a group that contains different objects that can be toggled between hidden and visible. These are useful for keeping your map organized and reducing visual clutter.

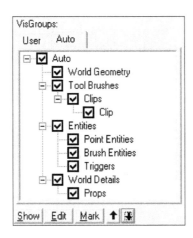

The **VisGroups** toolbar is located to the right of the four viewport windows. There are two tabs available for organizing your **VisGroups**: **User** and **Auto**. The **User** tab contains all the **VisGroups** that you create, while the **Auto** tab organizes all the individual items into lists so you can activate and deactivate them whenever you'd like.

With the example map loaded, turn of all **VisGroups** except for **World Geometry** to see what the world is made of.

You should see something similar to the preceding screenshot. Note that on the left-hand side, you can see the all the entities and special brushes. However, on the right-hand side, you only see the floor, walls, and ceiling. If your map is getting cluttered, try turning off some specific **VisGroups** to make your life easier. **VisGroups** will affect the 2D view as well as the 3D view.

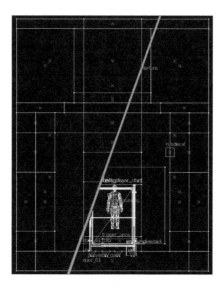

If you would like to create your own VisGroup, select a group of objects and go to **View** | **Move Selection to Visgroup**. Alternatively, you can hit the Move to VisGroup button on the toolbar at the top of the screen. It looks like a cube with red dotted lines (outlined in a red box in the following screenshot):

Summary

Navigating in all the viewports is simple once you get the hang of it, and it's vital to be comfortable with your mapping environment if you want to create spectacular maps. In the 3D view, you can use only the mouse, the mouse and Space bar, or the left mouse button and *W*, *S*, *A*, and *D* controls to get around. The 2D viewports can be easily navigated using a combination of mouse wheel zoom, Space bar and the left mouse button panning. Selecting objects is as simple as clicking on them in either view, and if you want to keep your map organized, VisGroups are the way to do it! The next chapter puts these tools to use. So now that you know how to get around, let's start creating!

3
Shaping Your World

Now that you're comfortable with getting around in Hammer, let's dive into the actual world creation. In this chapter, you will learn:

- Creating a house with world brushes
- Performing a test compile to view your work in the game
- Using the following tools:
    - **Clipping Tool**
    - **Carve**
    - **Vertex Tool**
- Using the object bar
- Creating a 3D SkyBox

Let us begin.

Creating your first room

The easiest way to get started with mapping is to dive right in and start! We know now that the most important thing about making a map with the **Source** engine is that we must completely seal of the world from the void. The easiest way to accomplish this is by starting with a hollow cube.

Select the **Block Tool**, and in the Top 2D viewport, drag out a box that is 1024 x 1024 units. In another 2D viewport (side or front), stretch the box so it is 1024 units tall and then press *Enter* to create a brush with those dimensions.

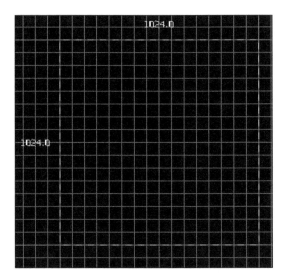

Congratulations! You have made your first brush. It will be textured with the currently selected texture.

Right now we have a solid cube. Let's make it hollow so that we can build inside it and use it to seal our map. Select your brush (if it isn't selected already) and navigate to **Tools | Make Hollow**.

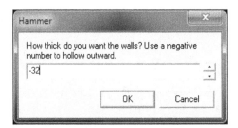

The **Hollow Tool**, as you would have guessed already, allows you to hollow out a brush. The tool will create walls with a specified depth inside the cube. So if you started with a 1024 x 1024 x 1024 cube and hollowed it out, the internal dimensions will be *less* than 1024 x 1024 x 1024. If you make the numbers negative, the internal dimensions stay the same while the walls expand outside the box. In this example, let's expand the walls outside so that the inside remains a 1024 unit box. Type in a negative value, such as -32, and click on **OK**.

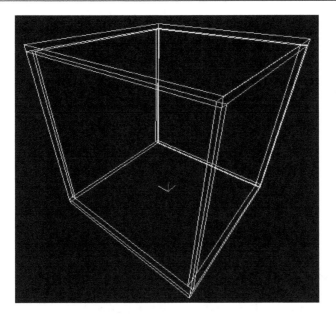

We now have a hollow box! Anything we place inside this box is going to be a part of this world. I know you're probably excited to jump in and play around in your map, so why don't we do a quick test compilation before we go any further?

A crash course on compiling

Every map needs three things in order to compile and play properly. They are:

- A sealed-off world for the player to move around
- A player start entity that defines where you start
- Light entities so we can see the world

We have already created a hollow cube, so we have the sealed-off world part covered. Now, we just need a player_start entity and a light entity. Both of these entities are **point** entities and are created with the **Entity Tool**. Grab your Entity Tool from the **Maptools bar** (the knob icon between the **Camera Tool** and Block Tool).

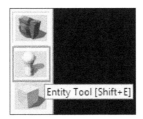

In the 3D view, left-click on any two random spots on the floor. This will create two copies of the default point entity at those points. With the **Selection Tool**, double-click on (or select it and press *Alt+Enter*) one of the entities you have just created to access the **Object Properties**. In the **Class** field, type info_player_start and hit the **Apply** button.

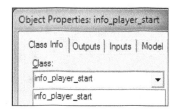

It might be pretty obvious, but the player will spawn at this location when the map starts. This map still needs a light. With the properties window still open, click on the other entity you have placed to bring up its properties. Turn this entity into a light by finding **light** in the dropdown, or by typing light. Again, hit **Apply** to save your changes and then close the **Object Properties** window. Move the light about 128 units above the middle of the floor in order to adequately light the room. We have now finished creating everything that a map needs to run! Unfortunately, we can't just open the map in Half-Life2 and run around, it needs to be compiled first. Hit *F9*, or click the compile icon in the top toolbar in order to build the map and prepare it for in-game use.

If you have not already saved your map, Hammer will prompt you to enter a filename for the map and a disk location to save your map onto.

Do not use spaces in your filenames. We can use the underscore (_) instead.

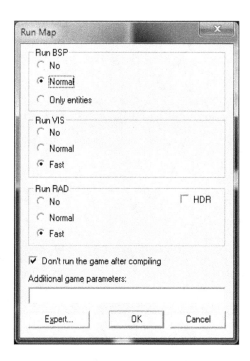

After saving (or if you have saved already), the compile window will appear. Let's just do a quick compile so **Run BSP** under **Normal**, and **Run VIS** and **Run RAD** under **Fast**. Disable **HDR** if it is enabled and check **Don't run the game after compiling**. It's easy to forget if you already have HL2.exe running and you will get an error if you try to launch the game while it's already running. When you click on **OK**, a console window will appear and the build programs will display the current compilation progress.

Once the compile finishes, launch your game (*Half-Life2: Episode 2* in my case) and open the command console with the tilde (~) key. Type in the command map mapname and press *Enter* to run your map. If, for example, your map is called my_map, type map my_map and then press *Enter*.

If you can't open the developer console, it hasn't been enabled yet.
To enable it, navigate to **Options | Keyboard | Advanced | Enable Developer Console**.

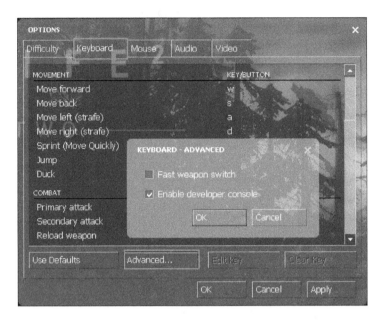

Congratulations! You have built and played around your very first Source map! Six walls with a simple light source can get boring pretty fast, so let's see what else we can do.

 If you would like to keep Half-Life 2 running while you develop, you need to at least exit your map. When you're ready to get back to mapping, type `disconnect` into the console to exit the map without closing Half-Life 2. If you compile the map when it's still open in Half-Life 2, weird things will happen and you will likely need to restart the game to get things back to normal.

Basic brushwork techniques

You've learned how to hollow out a cube, but that was just to whet your appetite. Let's create a little building in the center of our cube and learn some basic techniques along the way.

Cloning brushes

Let's make some walls for our building. Instead of using the Block Tool to specify an area, we can save some time and just copy and scale an existing brush to create another wall. We're going to select one of the walls of the cube we have just made. You'll notice that when you select one of the walls, all of them are selected. This is because when the **Hollow Tool** is used, it automatically groups the brushes it creates. To ungroup a group, you can click on the ungroup button in the top toolbar, or use the keyboard shortcut *Ctrl + U*.

Conversely, if you would like to group objects, click on the group button located to the left of the ungroup button, or you can use the keyboard shortcut *Ctrl + G*.

Now that our six walls are not grouped, you can select any individual wall. Select a vertical wall and while holding *Shift*, left-click on the wall and drag it to create a copy. If you release *Shift* too soon, the wall will just move and not copy, so make sure to release *Shift* only *after* you let go of the left-click mouse button.

 Cloning brushes is the fastest and easiest way to create copies of objects. The good-old copy paste method works as well, but using this technique will save you lots of time in the long run.

Scaling brushes and objects

You'll notice that when you have a brush selected, there are eight white boxes next to the brush. These white boxes are called **handles** and they allow you to manipulate the brush based on which selection mode is active. The **Scaling** mode is the default manipulation mode when any object is selected. In the Scaling mode, the corner handles allow you to scale, or stretch, a brush in two dimensions. The handles in the middle of an edge allow you to scale in one direction, perpendicular to the edge. So if a handle next to a vertical edge is selected, you will be able to scale a brush horizontally; and a horizontal edge handle allows vertical Scaling.

Select the brush you just copied, and in the front 2D viewport, scale it down to 128 units high and 8 units wide with the bottom of the brush touching the floor.

 Remember to change your grid size. The grid size increases with *]* and decreases with *[*.

In the Half-Life 2 World, 128 units is the average wall height and 8 units thick is an acceptable wall thickness.

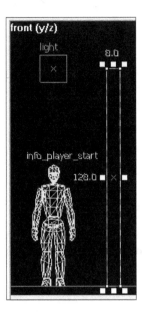

In the top or side view, stretch the brush so it's 512 units long. This is one of the long walls in our building. Now in the front viewport, *Shift* + copy the brush 256 units to the left to create two parallel walls that are 512 units long and 256 units apart.

Rotating brushes and objects

To make the connecting walls of our building, we could clone and then scale them, but let's learn how to **rotate** objects. Make another copy of a brush, and while it is still selected, left-click on it to change the manipulation mode. The eight box handles will change to four hollow circle handles located at the corners. This means you are in the rotate mode.

This can be seen in the following screenshot:

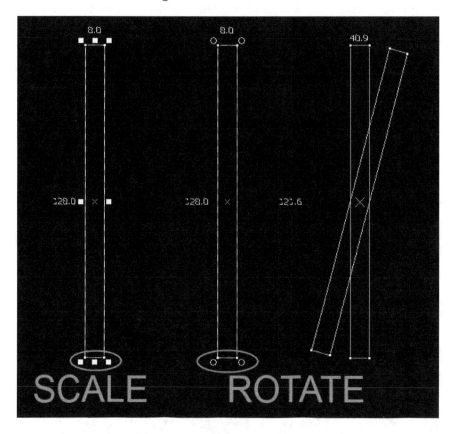

In the top view, rotate the brush by 90 degrees.

By default, Hammer is set up to snap up to 15 degree angles. If you would like more accuracy when rotating, hold the *Alt* key to disable the auto-snap function. The auto-snap amount can also be changed in the Hammer settings.

Keep in mind that the vertices of rotated objects will probably not align to the grid. You could end up with a leak if you use rotated brushes for world-sealing brushes.

Now left-click on the brush until you're back in the **Scale** mode, (left-click twice or until the eight box handles appear) and scale the brush to fit inside our long walls. Place one wall at one end of the long walls, and clone that wall to the opposite side. Voila! You have now created four standard-issue walls. Your viewports should look something like the following:

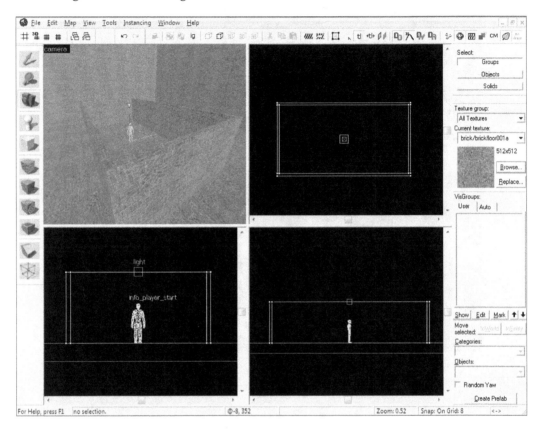

Skewing brushes and objects

No building is complete without a functioning roof. We could just throw a flat slab on top of the four walls and call it a day, but what's the fun in that? Let's create a classic pitched or slanted roof. In the front view, clone one of the long walls up, rotate it by 90 degrees, and scale it to make it half the width of the house. Align the bottom-right corner of the roof segment to the top-right edge of the house as seen in the following screenshot:

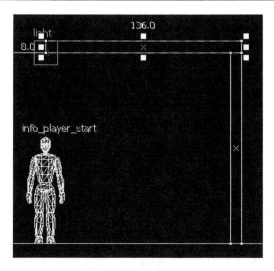

Now click on the object until four white handles appear on the sides of the brush. This brush is now in the **Skew** mode. Skewing an object moves a face parallel to its orientation and will turn a rectangle into a parallelogram. In the following example, the brush on the left was copied to the right and then the top edge was skewed to the right:

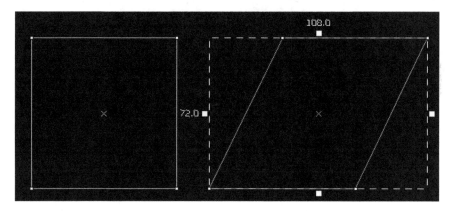

Skew the flat roof segment up from the left handle until the total height is around 100 units.

 The skew tool does not always snap the vertices to the current grid unit. This can cause off-grid vertices and might cause a leak! If this happens, clean up the corners using the **Vertex Tool**. Sometimes it's easier to use the Vertex Tool to save time.

Flipping objects

Now that we have one section of our roof built, we can copy and flip it to create the other half. Now clone the half roof to the other side of the house and press *Ctrl + L*. This will flip the object about the vertical axis, or left to right. You can also flip objects by going to **Tools | Flip Objects**. Once the second half of the roof is flipped, align it to the first half to complete your roof.

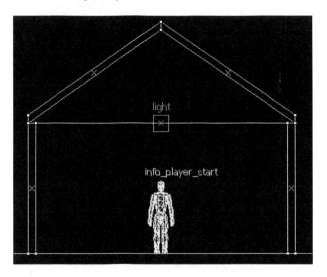

The Vertex Tool

We have created a roof, but there is still a gap that needs to be filled in between two of our walls. While we're at it, let's fix the ugly gap between the roof segments and the long walls. We can fix all of these issues easily with the Vertex Tool. This tool allows you to manipulate the vertices of brushes, and is also known as the **Vertex Manipulation Tool** or **VM Tool**. With the left roof segment selected, grab the VM Tool from the tools palette. The VM Tool looks like a gray wireframe cube with red vertices and can also be selected by pressing *Ctrl + V*. You'll notice that our selected roof segment now has eight square handles. There is a white handle on each vertex and a yellow handle on each edge. Clicking on the VM Tool icon (or pressing the keyboard shortcut *Ctrl + V*) will cycle through the VM modes. The standard mode allows both edges and vertices to be selected, but there are modes to manipulate only vertices and only edges.

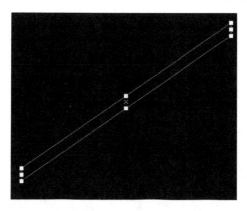

Let's manipulate some vertices! Moving vertices is as simple as left-clicking on one and moving it. If you are looking straight down the side of a brush and select a white handle, you are selecting the entire edge because any vertex directly underneath your selection will also be selected. So it's not necessary to select both vertices, since the one beneath it is already selected. The same thing goes for the yellow handles. Selecting a yellow handle will select the whole face if there is another yellow handle directly beneath it.

[If you want to select only one vertex, you need to drag a selection box around the target vertex in any two of the 2D viewports.]

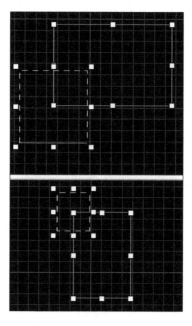

Move the lowest vertex on the left side to the inside top of the wall beneath it, and move the vertex above that to the outside edge of the wall.

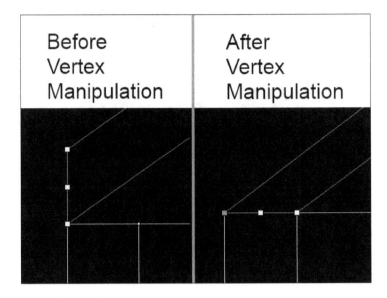

Now that our roof is aligned with the outside and inside of the house, it not only looks neater, but this also makes our lives easier when we go to raise the outer wall to the inside peak of the house. You can repeat this change to the other side of the house, or delete the other brush and then copy and flip the left brush over to the right side.

We can raise the outer walls up to the peak in a number of ways, but one of the quickest ways is to split the top face of the wall and bring the new edge up to the peak.

Splitting faces

We can split faces easily with the Vertex Manipulation Tool. Select one of the walls under the peak, and with your VM Tool, select the top face of the brush by clicking on the yellow handle.

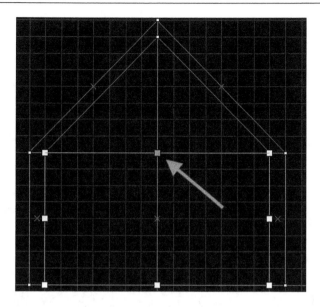

Press *Ctrl + F* to split the top face into two segments. You'll notice that the yellow handle has now turned into a white handle and two yellow handles have appeared on either side of the newly created middle white handle.

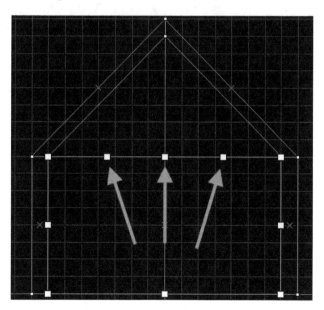

Select the newly created edge (middle white handle) and drag it up to the bottom of the roof peak.

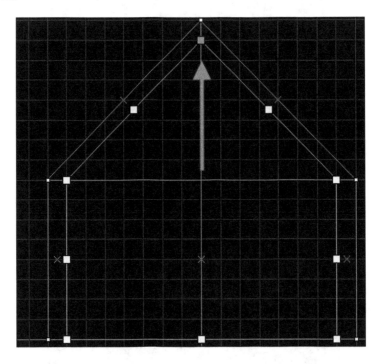

 Although splitting faces is a great way to give a brush many faces, be aware that all brushes still need to be convex! Also note that an object with two faces in a single plane will create an invalid solid.

Once you have mirrored the changes to the other brush, you're finished with your house! Now would be a good time for a test compilation.

The Clipping Tool

So now we have a house with no doors and no windows. Let's split one of these brushes and provide an entrance to our lovely home. The **Clipping Tool** will clip (cut) parts of a brush off, or split a brush into two sections; the icon resembles a cube with one of the edges cut or chamfered off. You can also press *Shift* + X to select the Clipping Tool. You need to select the brush you want to clip *before* you select the Clipping Tool because you cannot select an object with the Clipping Tool selected! Select one of the long walls in our house and then select the Clipping tool. Drag a vertical line in the middle of the brush where you want it to be split.

The clip line is defined by two white handles connected by a light blue line. The clip line extends along the entire selection so it's not necessary to perfectly align the handles with the edges of an object, but it is good practice because it will help prevent off-grid vertices.

Notice that one half of the brush is red and the other half is white. When you press *Enter*, the red half will be deleted and the white half will remain. Since we want to just split the wall without deleting anything, keep pressing the Clipping Tool icon (or the keyboard shortcut *Shift + X*) until both halves of our wall are white. Then press *Enter* to cut the wall in half.

A quick way to make a door in a wall is to clip the wall vertically twice, and drag the bottom of the middle brush up to where you want the top of the door to be.

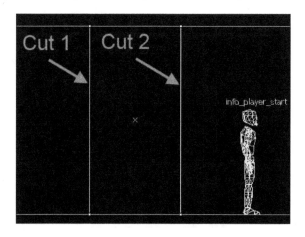

Using this method, create a door 64 units wide and 112 units tall. Use the player start entity as a reference scale. Since the wall height is 128 units, the brush at the top of the door will be 16 units tall and 64 units wide.

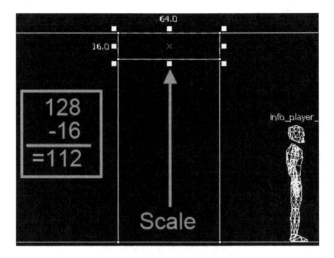

There you go! You now have a way to enter and exit your house. Why don't you give the map another test compile and check out your handiwork.

The Carve function

Now that we have a house with a door in one wall, let's put up a few windows so we can see the outside environment without actually walking outside. The **Carve Tool** works by overlapping two brushes and hitting the carve button on the toolbar. The selected brush will delete any sections of any brush it touches and make a group with the new brushes it has created.

 Caution! The carve function should *never* be used on anything other than a rectangle. It's known to create sloppy brushwork and create micro leaks, leaks smaller than one unit wide. Micro leaks are very hard to find and fix!

We're going to create a new brush to carve with this time around, so grab the Block Tool and make a 64 x 64 x 64 unit cube. Align the new cube brush with the center of one of the five sided walls on the short side of the house. With the cube selected, press the carve button located in the top toolbar.

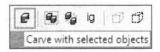

After the carve operation is complete, delete the cube and marvel at the mess you have made. If you aligned the top of the cube to the top of one of the vertical sides, you got lucky and your brushwork will be clean. But if you placed the top of the cube above that threshold, you might have something that looks like the following:

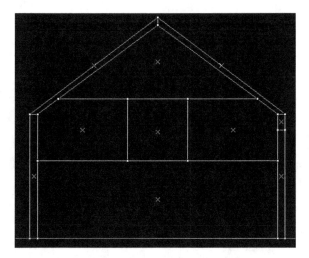

You're probably thinking "this doesn't look like a mess", but if you closely inspect the brushes that Hammer has automatically created you might think differently. Lower your grid size to one (the minimum) and check out the intersection of the horizontal line and the slant of the roof. The vertices are not on grid!

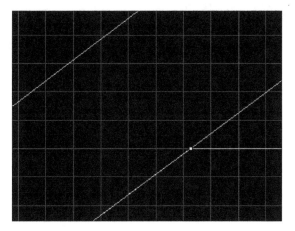

When the map compiles, all the off-grid vertices are rounded to the nearest unit. This can create some unwanted effects, and if the carved brush is meant to be a map-sealing brush, you could probably create a leak! It's good practice to only carve rectangles with rectangles. Carving is okay for windows, doors, and other rectangular objects, but the results get messy quickly when you have more than four sides in the equation. Take the following example of a twelve-sided cylinder carved into a square. Which group of brushes would you rather work with? Which group of brushes would you trust to be leak free?

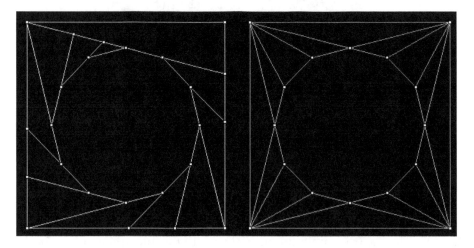

The group on the left was carved while the group on the right was vertex manipulated. Using Vertex Manipulation as we did in the preceding example will take some time and effort, but if your cylinders have an even number of sides, you will only have to do half of the work because you can copy half to the other side. Keeping your brushwork clean and on grid is one of the most important things you can do. If you spend some time now to keep things clean, you will save time in the long run, and your 2D views will be a lot less confusing.

Brushes can be used for some larger detail work, but the majority of fine details come from models. Models are easier for the engine to handle than standard brushwork, and the vertices don't have to be constrained to a grid.

Another window method

We know we can carve a hole in a wall to make windows, but we can clip windows in the same manner as the door we created earlier. Follow the same steps as before:

1. Make the brush rectangular if it is not.

2. Make two vertical cuts to the width of the window.

3. Make a horizontal cut into the newly created center brush.

4. Scale the top and bottom halves of the center brush to make the opening for your window.

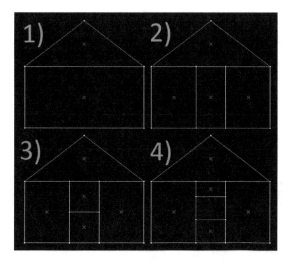

The Object Toolbar

So far, when we created brushes, we created blocks defined by an imaginary cube in 3D space. Hammer's default brush type is the block. But this can be changed by modifying the **Objects** property of the **Object Toolbar**.

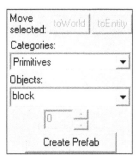

Click on the objects drop-down field to select either the **arch**, **block**, **cylinder**, **torus** (donut), **sphere**, **spike**, or a **wedge** object.

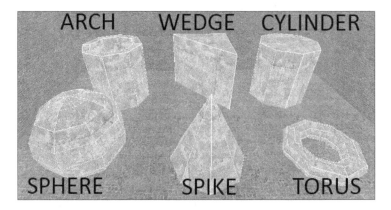

Creating cylinders

Cylinders are created by selecting **cylinder** from the **Objects** drop-down list. They're created just like boxes are except you specify how many sides you would like the cylinder to have.

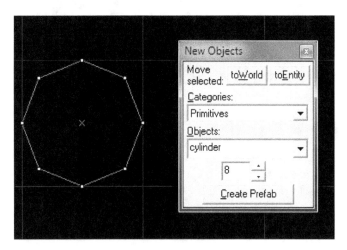

Upon creation, the top of the cylinder will face up, aligned with the z axis. This means that you will need to rotate the object to be in the final position you wanted. You can change which direction the object originally faces in the options menu. Navigate to **Tools | Options | 2D Views** and select the **Reorient primitives on creation in the active 2D view** option.

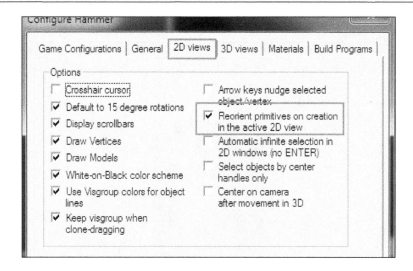

Cylinders, cones, arches, and tori will now face the active 2D view when created.

Creating small cylinders with too many sizes will create invalid objects. Take care when creating cylinders to avoid causing coplanar faces. Coplanar faces occur when two faces on one brush lie on the same plane. This will result in an invalid solid.

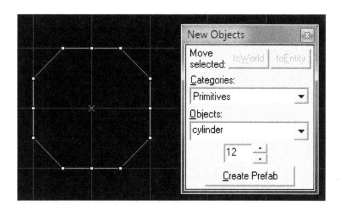

Creating spikes

Spikes, or cones, are created with the spike object tool and resemble cylinders with the top face meeting at a point in the center. Their creation is exactly like that of cylinders. Select the number of sides you wish your spike to have, drag a creation box, and press *Enter*. And this is how the result will look:

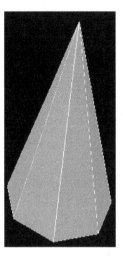

Truncated cones

To create a truncated cone, or a cone with the top cut off, you can clip the top off a cone with the Clipping Tool or you can scale the vertices. To do this, start with a cylinder and select all the vertices on one end with the Vertex Tool.

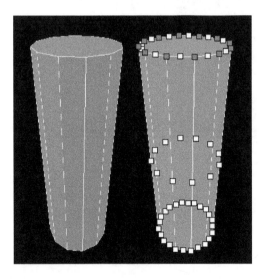

With the top side's vertices still selected, press *Alt + E* to bring up the Scale Tool. Use the up and down arrows to increase or decrease the scaling factor or type in any number you want.

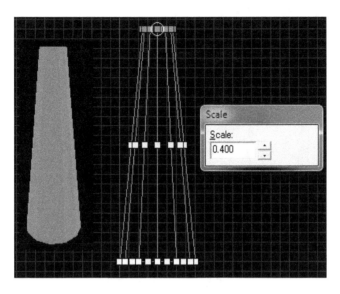

Creating a sphere

Spheres are created just like cylinders. Drag a creation box with **sphere** selected in the **Objects** toolbar and press *Enter*. Hammer will create a sphere within the box that has the number selected squared for faces. If you wanted a six-sided sphere, it will have 36 faces. If you selected an eight-sided sphere, it will have 64 faces. Keep in mind that these created primitives might be invalid structures. If so, they will not render properly in the game.

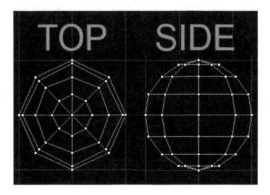

Make sure to check for problems, *Alt + P*, before doing a compile to make sure you are not creating any errors in your geometry. If the sphere is invalid, it will not render properly in the game and the compile time will increase dramatically. Check out the following screenshot to see how the sphere looks in the game with the `mat_wireframe 3` command:

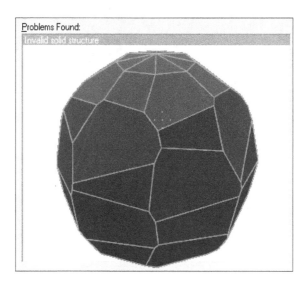

Creating arches

The tool used to create arches can be very useful. You can create standard arches, hollow cylinders, and even spiral staircases!

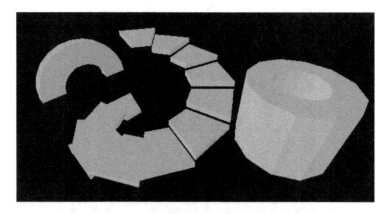

The box that controls the number of sides can be ignored as you will set more properties later. Select **Arch** from the drop-down list, drag a box, and press *Enter* to bring up the **Arch Properties** window:

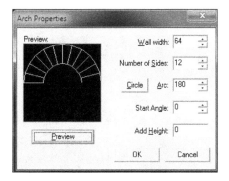

The **Arch Properties** window gives you five settings to play with as well as a preview window depicting the final outcome. At any point, click on the **Preview** button to update the preview window with your current values. **Wall width** controls how thick the arch walls will be upon creation. This value increases from the outer bounds toward the center of the arch. **Number of Sides** controls how many sides the arch has and **Arc** controls how far the arch spans. The **Circle** button will automatically fill the **Arc** property with a value of **360**, creating a closed circle. The arch's **Start Angle** defaults to **0** with the zero point facing east. The angle will increase counter clockwise. The **Add Height** property will give additional height to each arch segment starting from the zero point. Manipulating this property will let you create spiral staircases.

Standard arch

A standard arch is created by setting the **Arc field** to **180** degrees and **Start Angle** to **0**.. Set **Wall width** equal to your supported wall height, leave **Add Height** as **0**, and click on **OK** to create an arch!

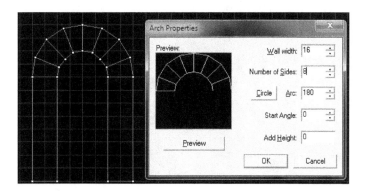

Hollow cylinders

Hollow cylinders are relatively easy to make as they're just closed (circular) arches. Set the desired values in the **Wall width** and **Number of Sides** fields and click on the **Circle** button to force a closed arch. Click on **OK** to marvel at your results!

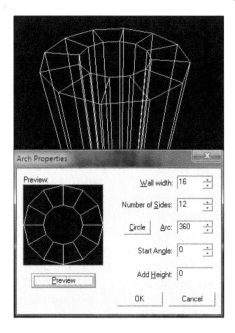

Spiral staircase

Spiral staircases would take a long time to create without the **Arch Properties** window. In this example, I will be creating a 180 degree stone staircase with 96 unit wide stairs and a step height of 12 units.

In order for our stairs to be created properly, the bounding box has to be square with each side at least twice as wide as our desired stair width. Start by creating a bounding box with the dimensions 256 x 256 x 12. Make sure to set the height of your bounding box equal to your step distance. Modifying the individual stairs after the staircase is created can take a long time.

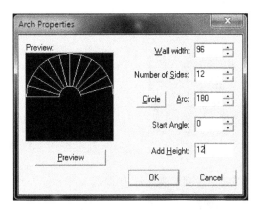

My **Arch Properties** are as follows: **Wall width** of 96, **Number of Sides** set to 12, **Arc** set to 180, **Start Angle** of 0, and **Add Height** set to 12. Remember, the **Add Height** field sets our step distance and not our stair height. The stair height is set by the original bounding box. Click on **OK** and check out your beautiful staircase!

The stair height does not have to equal the step distance (the distance in the **Add Height** field). For example, if you're making a metal staircase, the stair height is rather thin compared to the step distance. Keep this in mind as you create your staircases.

Creating a torus

A torus can be thought of as a donut or inner tube. Source can very rarely create these objects without creating a slew of invalid solids, but they're a fun shape to play around with. Let's create a torus tunnel for our player to walk around in.

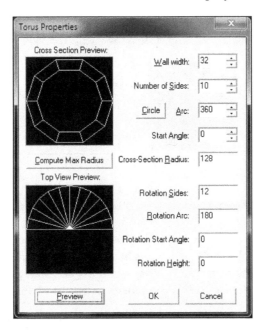

The **Torus Properties** window is very similar to the **Arch Properties** window, yet there are quite a few more values to edit. This tool can be considered an arch tool within an arch tool. It might be daunting at first glance, but you can break it down into two parts: **Cross Section Preview** and **Top View Preview**.

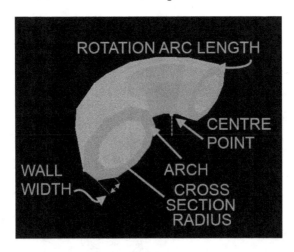

Cross Section Preview

The **Cross Section Preview** is laid out almost exactly like the standard **Arch Properties** window. You specify the values for the **Wall width**, **Number of Sides**, **Arc**, and **Start Angle** fields just like **Arch Properties**. There is no **Add Height** option; however, there is something similar in the **Top View Preview** portion. Think of it as the cross section arch being revolved around a center point.

Top View Preview

Again, just like the **Cross Section Preview**, there are properties for **Rotation Sides**, **Rotation Arc**, and **Rotation Start Angle**. But these apply to the revolution of the arch around the center point. If you want an open torus similar to a piece of elbow macaroni, choose a rotation angle of 180 degrees.

Springs

You can create a spring with the **Torus Tool** by specifying a value in the **Rotation Height** field. This will apply to the end segment's height above the first segment. To create a coiled spring, simply copy and paste the torus.

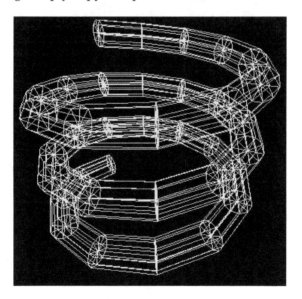

 Remember that most tori will create many invalid solids. You can fix them from the **Check for problems** window, but they will probably not retain their original shape. Regardless, tori should be tied to entities such as func_detail to ease the stress on the engine.

Creating SkyBoxes

An important part of any map is the **sky**. In Source, the sky is called a **SkyBox**, and it helps give the illusion that you're standing in a world that is bigger than what is really there. There are two types of Skyboxes available in Source: the **2D SkyBox** and the **3D SkyBox**. Let's have a look at them.

2D SkyBox

The 2D SkyBox is comprised of six images displayed on an infinitely large cube around the outside of the level. Let's set up a quick 2D SkyBox in our current map and we will see how it works. Select the four vertical walls of your giant box and using the Clipping Tool, cut them in half horizontally as shown in the following figure:

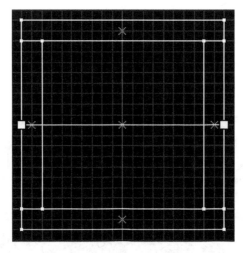

Select the ceiling and the top four sections of the walls you just clipped. We're going to apply a special texture to these brushes in order to form our SkyBox.

Select the **texture tool** from the tools palette, or hit *Shift* + *A*. The texture tool looks like a green, red, and blue cube.

Once the texture tool appears, hit the **Browse...** button to bring up the texture browser. Locate the filter entry in the bottom toolbar and type in `toolsSkyBox`; you'll see two textures appear. One texture is a 2D SkyBox and the other is a 3D SkyBox. Left-click on it twice or hit *Enter* with the 2D SkyBox texture (**tools/toolsSkyBox2D**) selected to set it as the current texture. When the texture browser closes, notice that the 2D Skybox texture is displayed in the texture preview pane.

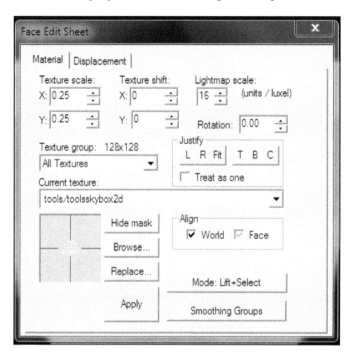

Click on the **Apply** button to paint our selected brushes with the 2D SkyBox texture. The SkyBox texture has a special function that other textures don't have, but it still seals our world off from the void so there is no need to place other brushes behind it. Let's do a test compile to see the results of our new 2D SkyBox. When in the game, you'll notice that there is now a cloudy sky behind our tall walls. Also, notice that the whole area looks very strange because the sky isn't projecting any light into our map. SkyBoxes have the ability to cast light but we need to add in a special light entity to make that happen.

Adding light_environment

With the Entity Tool, place a **light_environment** class anywhere in the map. Let's open the properties and take a look:

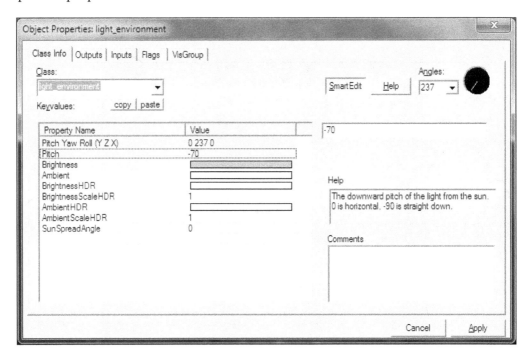

There are many properties we can edit, but right now we're only concerned about three: **Pitch**, **Angles**, and **Brightness**.

The **Pitch** property is the vertical projection of light from the SkyBox texture; -90 will project light straight down, 0 will project light horizontally, and 90 will project light straight up. Set the **Pitch** property to something below 0, but greater than -90; I prefer **Pitch** values around -70 for a nice midday effect.

The **Angles** property will control which direction the light will project if you're looking down on your map. A good way to set your desired angle is to place the **Object Properties** window above the top 2D viewport, and set the angle by clicking inside the black circle. The white line inside the black circle will depict which direction light will shine out of the 2D SkyBox texture.

The **Brightness** property controls not only the brightness of our light but the color as well. Since our default SkyBox has a greyish blue hue to it, let's try to match the projected light color to the SkyBox color for a more realistic scene. You'll notice four three-digit numbers in the entry field when you select the **Brightness** property:

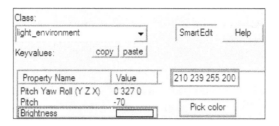

The first three numbers control the light color in **RGB** (Red, Green, and Blue) format. Thankfully, we don't need to know how to set a color in the RGB format and we can just click on the **Pick Color** button to select any color we want. The last number in the brightness value controls the actual light intensity or brightness. This last number can be left at 200 as this is a decent starting value.

Compile your map and take a look! You'll notice that the sky is projecting a light onto your map! Now what if we don't like this depressing cloudy day SkyBox? We can change it quite easily.

Changing the SkyBox texture

Open up the texture browser and type in SkyBox into the filter. The page should flood with cloudy sky pictures. You'll notice that there are groups of six images that all look similar. They all share similar names as well. The naming convention can be confusing at first glance, but it is really just the sky name with a suffix of which face it's supposed to be. So let's look at the sky texture called **SkyBox/sky_day01_08_hdrlf**.

The SkyBox name is **sky_day01_08_hdrlf** and **lf** tells us that this image is being projected onto the left part of the sky. If we would like to use this sky for our map, we need to set the **Skybox Texture Name** property in the **Map Properties**. To get to the **Map Properties**, go to **Map | Map Properties**.

Skybox suffix naming convention: **lf** projects left, **rt** projects right, **ft** projects forward, **bk** projects backward, **up** projects up, and **dn** projects down.

With our SkyBox name set, give your map another compile to see what it looks like. Feel free to change the **light_environment** color to reflect the new color of the SkyBox light.

3D Skybox

The 3D SkyBox will project light into our map just like the 2D SkyBox did, but it also allows us to project objects and models into the scene. The 3D SkyBox is created around your level, shrunk to a fraction of its normal size, and then blown up and projected around your map when you run it in the game. This might sound confusing, but let's just take it one step at a time; we'll get there.

First, shrink the top and bottom sections of your vertical walls to 256 units each, and then bring the ceiling sky texture down on top of the vertical sky sections. Select everything in the current map and create a visgroup with it. Name it something useful such as house in a box. Making this part of the map into a visgroup is going to make our lives easier in a moment.

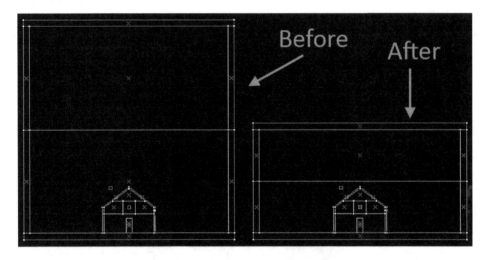

Now create a 1600 x 1600 x 1056 unit block. Center the new brush on your existing map but have the bottom of the new brush touch the bottom of the floor. Hollow the new brush out with a value of -32 so the walls grow outward and we keep our inner dimensions. We should now have a new box surrounding our old box that is surrounding a house.

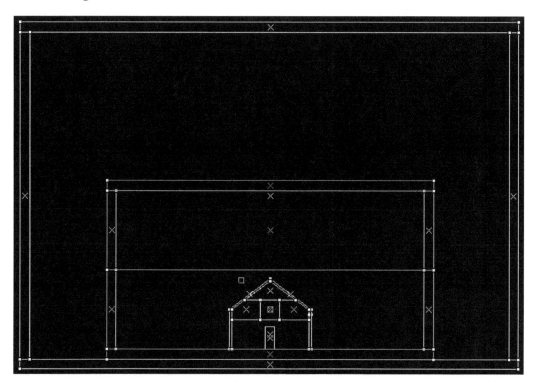

Since we're making a 3D SkyBox now, we need to change the tool texture we're using. Select the newly hollowed box as well as the 2D SkyBox-textured brushes that make up the outer enclosing walls. Launch the texture application tool, browse for textures, and filter for tools/toolsSkyBox. Hit *Enter* to select the 3D SkyBox texture, and then hit **Apply** in the texture application tool to paint all the selected brushes with the **toolsSkyBox** texture. The tools/toolsSkyBox texture is the one we need to create 3D SkyBoxes.

Now we need to populate the 3D SkyBox with some buildings. For simplicity's sake, let's not get too detailed in the 3D SkyBox just yet. Just make some tall rectangular brushes and randomly place them around our map in between the outer SkyBox walls and the house in a box.

Place an entity called **sky_camera** at the map's origin (0, 0, 0).

 The **sky_camera** entity needs to be placed at the map's origin before the SkyBox can be moved. The **sky_camera** entity references the map's origin and tells the engine where to base the projection around in the game.

We now have all the items necessary for the SkyBox to project properly, but we're not done yet; we need to scale the SkyBox down a bit. You'll notice in the **Object Properties** of **sky_camera**, there's a property called **3D Skybox Scale**. This is the number of times that the SkyBox will be blown up and projected around the map. By default, this value is at **16** and we're going to leave it at that. Now, remove visibility of the **house in a box** visgroup by unchecking the box next to it in the visgroup toolbar. Select everything else (in your SkyBox) and then turn it into a group with the toolbar button or by pressing *Ctrl + G*. This group is the SkyBox. Since our **sky_camera** scale is **16**, we need to scale this SkyBox down by a factor of **16**. A quick calculation tells us that one divided by 16 equals to 0.0625. This is the scale factor we need to apply to our SkyBox group. Select the SkyBox group and go to **Tools | Transform** (or hit *Ctrl + M*) to pull up the **Transform Tool**. The Transform Tool lets us precisely control the object scaling, rotation, or movement. Select the scale radio button and enter 0.0625 into each of the entry fields to scale the SkyBox evenly on all three axis. When you hit *Enter*, the SkyBox will now be 1/16th of its original size.

 Make sure to turn on texture scale lock if you want your scaled brushes to keep their original texturing effects. The texture scale lock button is located in the middle of the top toolbar and looks like this: **<-tl->** (tl in a box with two arrows coming out of it).

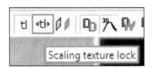

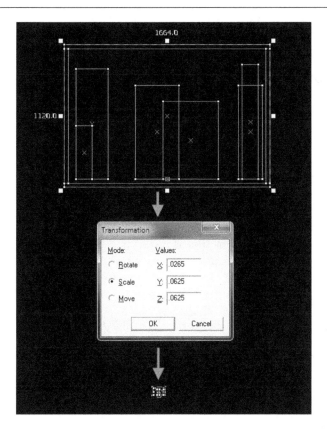

Congratulations! You have completed your first 3D SkyBox. Unhide the **house in a box** visgroup and place the SkyBox group far beneath the floor of the house in a box. Run a test compile and check out the results; they should look similar to the following:

Summary

You have learned to create brushes of all shapes and sizes with the box tool and object properties window, but you have also learned how to make quick copies of existing brushes with the cloning technique. When an object is selected in a 2D viewport, you can scale an object when there are eight white handles surrounding an object, rotate when there are four white circle handles surrounding an object, and skew when four white boxes surround an object. Flipping objects is a useful technique that can save time when making symmetrical creations; *Ctrl + L* flips horizontally while *Ctrl + I* flips vertically. The Vertex Tool is useful for making irregular brush shapes, but it's also useful to create new edges on a brush using the *Ctrl + F* command. The Clipping Tool is useful to cut parts of brushes or split brushes along a line. Remember that when a section of a brush is highlighted in white, it will be kept after it is clipped. If the section is red, it will be deleted. The carve technique is useful to put square holes in square objects. You can carve anything with anything but you're going to get some ugly brushwork as a result. 2D and 3D SkyBoxes are easy to create, and enhance the atmosphere and immersion in any map.

I bet you're getting tired of looking at this default brick texture. Let's learn how to use the texturing tool to its full potential.

4
Textures, Terrain, and Props

I bet you're pretty tired of that generic brick floor texture. Let's change things up a bit while learning how to navigate the texture tool. We can also bring more detail into the world with decals, overlays, displacements, and props!

In this chapter, you will be learning the following:

- Texturing techniques
- Placing decals and overlays
- Creating terrain with displacements
- Learning about the different prop types

Let's go!

Using the Texture Application Tool

Using the **Texture Application Tool** gives you full control over the application of textures in the Source engine. You can select, apply, scale, rotate, and align textures all within this easy-to-use tool.

Applying textures

There are many ways to apply textures to brushes. Brushes, upon creation, are given the currently selected texture, but there is still much to learn!

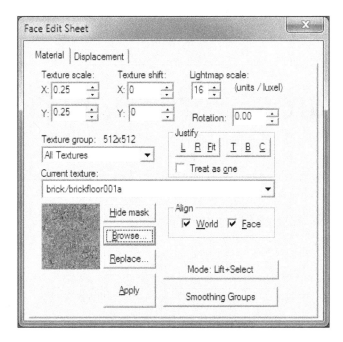

There are two main tabs in the Texture Application Tool. For now, let's focus on the **Material** tab. The first thing you'll probably notice about the Texture Application Tool is that the window title actually says **Face Edit Sheet**. Since the tool is named Texture Application Tool, that is what I'll be calling it throughout this chapter. The second thing you'll notice is the texture preview pane in the bottom-left corner. Just above this is the **Current texture** drop-down list that displays the current texture name and allows you to quickly select the last few textures you have used. Let's get acquainted with this tool by first selecting a new floor for us to walk on. Click on the **Browse** button to bring up the **Texture browser**.

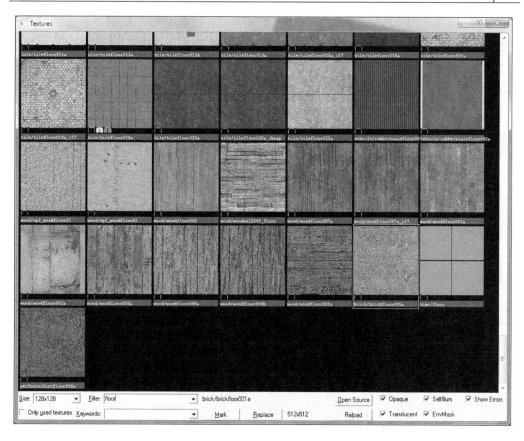

We're looking for a floor texture, so instead of scrolling through hundreds of images, we can just type in `floor` in the **Filter** field. The browser will update automatically as you type, so there's no need to hit *Enter*. If you do press *Enter*, you'll close the browser without selecting the texture you wanted. You'll notice that the texture preview size is relatively small. If you want to get a better look at the individual textures, you can change the display size in the the drop-down menu titled **Size** at the bottom-left corner. The checkbox under the size selector, **Only used textures**, will allow you to see only the textures currently used in our map; since we're browsing for a new texture, leave this unchecked. There are various other checkboxes in the bottom-right corner that filter for special material properties. We're looking for an opaque floor, so uncheck the rest of the checkboxes to make our search easier.

The **Opaque** flag displays all nontransparent textures, while the **Translucent** flag displays anything with an alpha channel. **Selfillum** displays any textures that are self-illuminated or emit light.

For the sake of following this tutorial, find the **stone/stonefloor_inn01** texture and press *Enter* to set it as the current texture and return to the Texture Application Tool.

 Just because this texture has the word floor in it doesn't mean we can't use it anywhere else. There is nothing stopping you from using a floor texture on a ceiling or a wall. Be creative!

Textures are best applied in the 3D view; so, in the 3D viewport, right-click on the floor to apply our cobblestone texture to the top face of the floor brush.

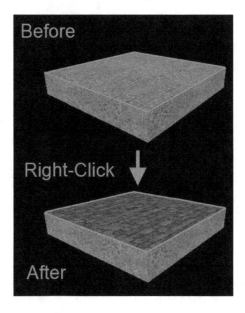

Each face can only have one texture applied to it at any time, so if you want another texture in the floor, we need to create another face to apply the texture to. Brushes cannot have more than one face on a single plane (or else you will get a nasty coplanar face error while compiling), so, if we want to detail the floor in the house, we need to clip the floor into multiple brushes.

Using the same technique used to make windows in *The Clip Tool* section of *Chapter 3*, *Shaping Your World*, clip the floor so that there's a middle section that aligns with the walls of the house. (You should end up with five brushes in total.)

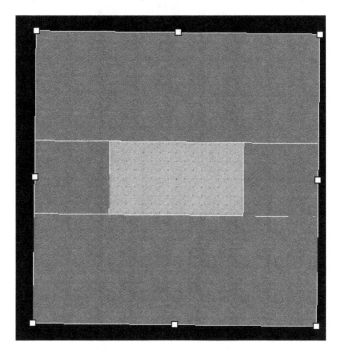

Return to the Texture Application Tool, open the texture browser and find a tile texture to apply to the floor; **tile/tilefloor011a** should do this nicely. Right-click on the house floor to apply the texture.

We could spend the next couple of minutes texturing each face individually, but you can also apply a texture to an entire brush or a group of brushes to save time. Exit the Texture Application Tool and select all the vertical walls of the house. Open the Texture Application Tool and then click on **Browse** to search for a wall texture. Find the texture titled **brick/brickwall014l**, select it, and press *Enter* to return to the Texture Application Tool. Click on the **Apply** button to apply the current texture to each face in the selection.

It's generally considered good practice to apply the **tools/toolsnodraw** texture, also known as **Nodraw**, to any brush face that will not be seen in the game. Faces with Nodraw applied to them will not be rendered in the game and will ease the load on the engine. To do this quickly, follow these steps:

1. Select a brush.
2. Open the Texture Application Tool.

3. Deselect the visible faces.

4. Apply Nodraw to the remaining faces.

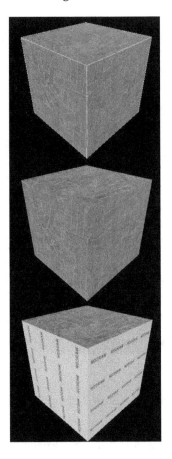

Aligning textures

The **Justify** section of the Texture Application Tool contains a few buttons to quickly align textures.

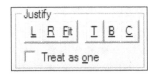

You'll notice that the textures aren't aligned nicely. That's where the **Justify** menu comes into play. With all your walls still selected, press the **B** button to align the bottom of the texture with the bottom of the brush.

Take a look at the brush on top of the doorway. Note that the textures are aligned to the bottom of the individual brushes. To remedy this situation, check the **Treat as one** checkbox and align the textures to the bottom again.

The **Treat as one** option tells Hammer to treat all the faces on the same plane as one large texture, and it will apply all changes to them as if they were one. You can probably guess that **T** aligns textures to the top edge, **L** aligns textures to the left edge, **R** aligns textures to the right edge, and **C** will center the texture on a face.

Let's check out the **Fit** functionality by creating a window. Open the texture browser and find the **glass/glasswindow017a** texture. Use the **block tool** to create a brush of the size and shape of one of the window openings. When you create a new block, the current texture will automatically be applied to the brush, so we don't have to apply it manually; we do, however, need to modify its appearance.

Open the texture tool and left-click on the outside face of the window to select only that face. The default texture scale is 0.25, but this doesn't work well for our window. Press the **Fit** button to stretch the texture across the entire face of the brush and calculate the X and Y texture scales.

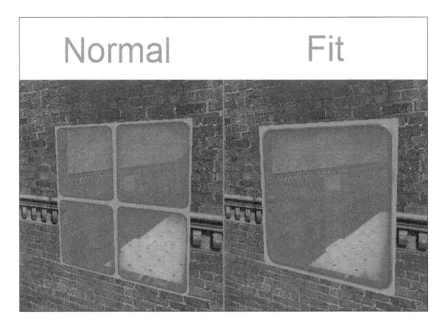

Fitting a texture to a brush can be a great technique. However, beware of larger texture values that will start to look stretched and blurry. Try using the **Fit** function on the tile floor inside of the house. It doesn't look too great, does it?

Shifting and rotating textures

Let's experiment with the texture shift and rotation tools by texturing our roof. Find the **metal/metalroof006** texture and apply it to the top and sides of the roof brushes. The new texture will inherit all the attributes of the old texture: scale, rotation, and alignment. When you apply the texture to the roof, it will be slightly stretched in the y direction because Hammer defaults to **World** texture projection. What this means is that the texture is projected onto the brush from the z axis. Since the roof is sloped against the z (vertical) axis, the texture will be stretched in one direction. If a face is parallel to the projection plane, the texture will be projected properly.

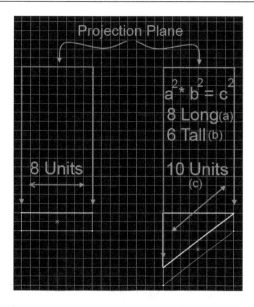

In the previous example, the projection plane is aligned perfectly on the left half of the page. But to the right, the texture plane is 20 percent larger than the projection plane. To eliminate this stretching effect, select the **Face** checkbox. This mode will ensure that the texture is always projected perpendicular to the face (as if you're staring straight at it)! So, after applying the metal roof texture to the roof, select both roof segments and click on the **Face** checkbox to ensure that the textures are projected properly.

Right-click on the sides of the roof brushes to apply the roof texture to them. Remember, the new texture will inherit all the attributes of the old texture, so the texture on the side of the roof brush will have vertical stripes.

Select the side of the roof texture and keep increasing the **Rotation** property until those vertical stripes are aligned with the slope of the roof. If you have been following my examples closely, a rotation of about 54 degrees should work well. Once you are satisfied with the rotation angle, left- or right-align the texture to clean things up.

Saving time while aligning textures

There's a much faster way to align textures between faces. This method does not have a specific name, but I call it the *Alt* + right-click method. With the Texture Application Tool active, select the top of the other roof brush. While holding *Alt*, right-click on the side of the roof brush to automatically wrap the texture around the brush edge onto the new face.

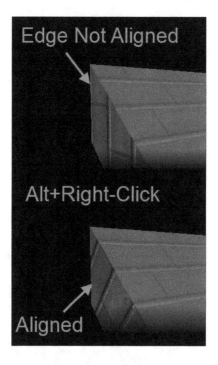

Voilà! This method of texturing is very useful and can save you hours of painstaking alignment and rotation.

Using different selection modes

So far, we have been using the default selection mode called **Lift and Select**. It's very useful for the *Alt* + right-click texturing method, and it's arguably the most flexible of the texture selection modes. With this tool, left-clicking on a face will set the face's texture to current as well as select the face. If you right-click on a face, the current texture will be applied to that face. There are other selection modes called **Lift**, **Select**, and **Apply**, but the **Lift and Select** tool contains all their functions. The **Apply (texture only)** tool will apply the current texture to the face that is clicked on, but the new texture will inherit the old texture's values. Conversely, the **Apply (texture and values)** tool will apply the current texture, scale, and rotation to the current face. There is a texture application mode called **Align to view**, which will rotate and skew the texture based on the camera's angle relative to the face; however, be careful with this mode because due to a bug in Hammer, you cannot undo a texture application.

Shifting textures

If you have already tried all the alignment options, or if you want a bit more control over the position of the texture, you have the option of shifting a texture on the x or y axis. Both x and y default to zero, but you can change that in three ways. Use the ramping arrows next to the numerical entry and type in your own value, or you can use the arrow keys on your keyboard to shift the texture by an amount equal to the current grid size.

Locking textures

Texture lock, by default, is enabled. When you move an object with texture lock enabled, the texture applied to that object will follow it. If texture lock is off, the texture will stay in place while the brush moves.

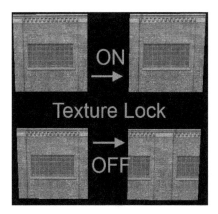

You can turn the texture lock on and off by clicking on the **tl** button in the menu bar on the top.

Locking the texture scale

Texture scale lock is another useful option. Located right next to the texture lock button, it will scale a texture relative to the brush it is applied to.

With the texture scale lock enabled, any brush you resize will keep the texture scale intact.

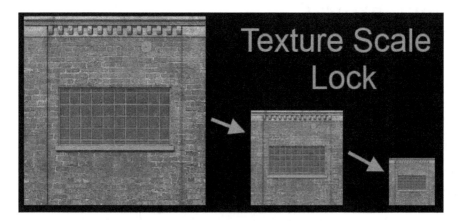

Applying decals

Decals are special textures that are placed on brushes to help break the monotony of a repeating texture or just to add small details. When you shoot a wall in the game, decals are applied to the places where the bullets hit. Unlike normal textures, they don't have to occupy an entire brush face. When a decal is placed in the 3D view, a point entity **infodecal** is placed at the mouse cursor's location, and the decal texture is projected onto all surfaces within 16 units of the **infodecal** origin.

Decals have special render properties that separate them from normal textures. It's not a good practice to apply a regular texture as a decal because the scaling is different. When a decal texture is placed with the decal tool, the texture is scaled down. This scaling is specified when creating the decal texture. When standard textures are applied, there is no scaling taking place. There's nothing stopping you from applying a standard texture as a decal or even creating a brush with a decal texture.

Open the texture browser and type `decals/` to filter all the available decal textures. Choose any decal you like and open the decal tool with *Shift + D* or by clicking on the decal tool on the tools palette (a brick cube with a target on one face).

To apply a decal, simply left-click on any face, and an **infodecal** entity will be created at that point. To adjust the location of the decal, move it around in the 2D view with the select tool. The decal texture can also be changed by opening the **infodecal** properties and choosing a different decal texture. Be careful when applying decals near wall intersections; the decals can affect more than one face at a time if placed within 3 units of an intersection. In the following screenshot, this idea is emphasized where the metal decals are one unit higher than its neighbor on the left.

The leftmost decal is right at the intersection of the two brushes. Once the decals are more than 3 units away from the nearest wall, the decals are only applied to that specific face.

This behavior can be used to your advantage if you want to depict, for instance, a bloodstain in a corner.

 Decals can be manually turned on by firing the **activate** output from a trigger. This can be useful for dynamically changing the look of a wall or simulating damage and blood splatter. They cannot be turned off because the entity is removed from the world once activated.

Applying overlays

Overlays are similar to decals but you can control the scale, rotation, and faces that they are applied to. With this greater power comes a greater cost; overlays take up a greater percentage of processing power as compared with a decal. However, they cannot be toggled on and off, so they will always stay where they are.

You place an overlay in the same manner that decals are placed—grab the overlay tool (a brick cube with grass top), select an overlay texture, and then click on a face in the 3D view to apply an overlay entity. Once an overlay is created, you can then modify the scale and rotation just like any normal brush in the 2D view. In the 3D view, you have control over each corner of the overlay. Move the corners around to change the shape of the overlay to suit your needs. Again, normal textures can be applied as overlays, but the end result might not be as expected.

Creating terrain with displacements

Terrain in the Source engine is created with objects known as displacements. Displacements are tessellated modifications of brush faces and are created within the texture tool.

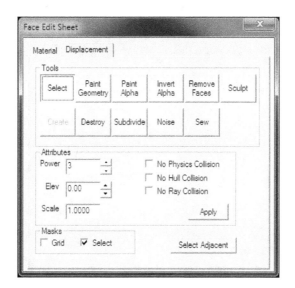

You've probably been wondering what that second tab in the texture tool is. The **Displacement** tab controls all the terrain features of Hammer. A displacement is the Source's version of terrain, and a displacement surface is created from a four-sided brush face. Unlike regular brushwork, displacements are sculpted almost entirely in the 3D viewport, and it does take some getting used to. There are some guidelines to remember while working with displacements:

- A displacement surface *must* have four and only four sides
- Displacements cannot be made into entities
- Displacements do not seal the world off from the void

Keeping these things in mind, let's start playing with displacements!

Creating a displacement

In the southeast corner of your map, create a block that spans the gap between the corner of the wall and the corner of your house that uses the **nature/blenddirtgrass001a** texture. Align the bottom of the new brush with the top of the floor and make the brush 8 units tall. Open the texture tool, and select the **Displacement** tab. Select the top face of the new brush, and select **Create** to make a new displacement surface.

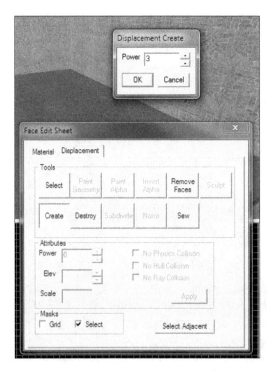

Displacements cut up the selected faces into triangles and discard any brush faces that are not selected. The number of triangles that are created per brush is controlled by the **Power** property. Powers of 2, 3, and 4 can be created, but in this example, let's keep the power at the default value of 3. The higher the power, the more faces in the displacement, and the more graphics horsepower you need to render them. Try to keep the numbers as low as possible while still maintaining the desired level of detail.

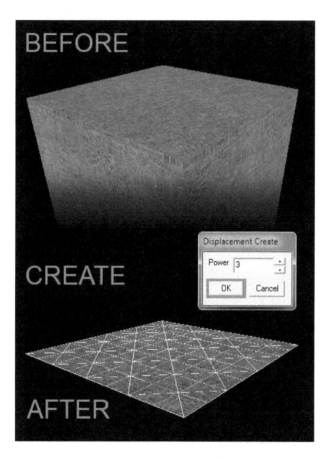

Once the **Power** field is set and the **OK** button is pressed, you'll notice that the new face is selected, the triangles are highlighted in white, and the nondisplacement faces of the brush have disappeared! Let's start sculpting some terrain.

Using the Paint Geometry tool

The **Paint Geometry** window holds the tools we need to modify the displacement surfaces.

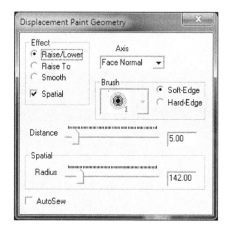

Click on **Paint Geometry** in the main displacement tab to open it. By default, the **Effect** option of the tool is **Raise/Lower**. This tool will raise or lower the displacement geometry by a distance specified with the **Distance** slider. The axis of effect can be selected with the **Axis** drop-down, and the radius of the displacement modification can be controlled in the **Spatial** section with the option to have a soft or hard edge. You might be overwhelmed by the sheer amount of options that you have, but everything is really quite simple to use. Let's jump in.

Change the **Axis** to **Z** so we can move the displacement surface along the vertical axis. With the **Radius** set around 140, and the **Distance** set to 5, left-click once on the middle of the new displacement surface to raise the surface by 5 units.

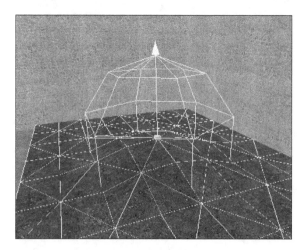

Note that your cursor turns into a gizmo with a green sphere of influence, a yellow box, and an arrow. The yellow box is the middle of the displacement area of effect, and it will snap to the vertices on the displacement mesh. The yellow arrow designates the axis on which the displacement will move. Left-clicking will move the vertex in the direction of the arrow, while right-clicking will move the vertex in the opposite direction. The green sphere designates the area of effect that your displacement modification will have. Any vertex inside the sphere of influence will move, while any vertex outside the sphere will remain stationary. If you want to move a single vertex, change the **Radius** to 0, or simply uncheck the **Spatial** checkbox.

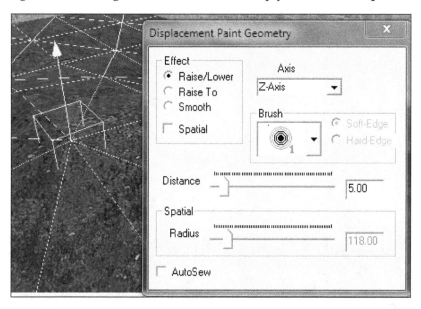

The displacement tool can be very sensitive at times. Holding the left or right mouse button down while moving the mouse over the displacement surface can have profound effects on your surface even with small distance values. If you would like to precisely position a point on your displacement surface, hold *Shift* and then left-click to drag a vertex along the specified axis. Moving the mouse up will move the vertex in the positive axis direction, while moving the mouse down will move the vertex in the negative axis direction.

Using the techniques learned so far, create a mound of dirt in the corner of the wall. Sink the outside edges of the displacement below the cobblestone brush face so that it looks like there's a natural transition between the stone and terrain.

 Remember, at any time, feel free to do a test compile of your map to check your progress!

We would probably like to walk on this surface when we're in the game. We can check to see if our displacement will allow movement. Click on the **Display Walkable Mask** button in the top toolbar to toggle the visibility of the nonpassable areas of your displacement.

Any area that cannot be walked on will now be highlighted in yellow:

It looks like I have some nonwalkable areas in my displacement that I want to fix. There are three ways I can fix this; using the **Raise/Lower** tool we just learned about, using the **Smooth** tool, or changing the displacement scale.

Using the Smooth tool

If you haven't guessed already, the smooth tool smoothens the displacement mesh. In general, it averages the displacement surfaces within the sphere of influence along the selected axis. If you want to smooth your mesh out a bit, select the smoothing tool and click once or twice on the area you wish to smooth. Again, the displacement tools can be sensitive, so a light touch is recommended.

Modifying the displacement options

Exit the paint geometry menu to get back to the displacement tab in the Texture Application Tool. On the left half of the **Attributes** section, you will see three numerical entry fields. The power, elevation, and scale can be changed here. The **Elev** property controls the base distance that the displacement surface is raised to in relation to the original brush face. The default is zero. The **Scale** property controls the effect of the displacement on the surface. If you wanted to keep the general shape of your displacement but change the amplitude of your changes, you can modify the scale. Scale values lower than 1 will subdue displacement changes, while scale values greater than 1 will exaggerate changes. In my case, since I have nonpassable parts of my displacement, I want to reduce the **Scale** factor of my displacement to 0.5. Click on the **Apply** button to apply any changes.

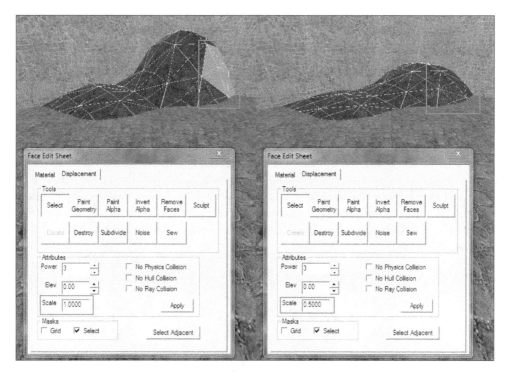

Using the Raise To option

Within the **Paint Geometry** window, the **Raise To** option will move all vertices within the sphere of influence to the distance offset from the original displacement face. Positive values will move the vertices up. Negative values will move the vertices below the original brush face. There is no falloff when using this tool, so the displacement edges are harsh and will probably need smoothing.

Using the Paint Alpha tool

Let's exit the **Paint Geometry** tool and check out the **Paint Alpha** tool. **Blend textures** have an **Alpha channel** that can be manipulated to fade or blend between two textures. The texture that we have created our displacement with is called **nature/blenddirtgrass001a**. Note that it has **blend** in the texture name. The **Paint Alpha** window allows you to control the blending between the two textures.

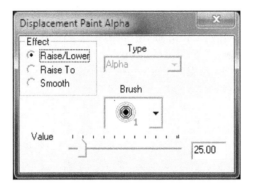

There is no sphere of influence in the **Paint Alpha** window, so the effect radius is controlled with the **Brush** dropdown. You can select a range between 1 and 5, and the alpha will have a **falloff** effect that starts at the center vertex and ends a number of vertices away as specified by the brush value. So, if you select 3 for a brush setting, the effect will be most apparent at the selected vertex and will fade out completely at the third vertex away in all directions. Left-click to add alpha to your displacement and right-click to remove alpha from your displacement. The **Smooth** and **Raise To** settings have the same effect as they did in the paint geometry window.

You can click on the **Invert Alpha** button in the main displacement window to flip the alpha channels of any selected face.

Sewing

Multiple displacements can be modified at once. This can be done with the following steps:

1. Hold *Shift* and drag this displacement to make a copy and align the east side of the copy to the west side of the original. You'll note that the two displacement edges are drastically different.

2. Select both the displacement surfaces and click on **Sew** in the main displacement window. All the vertices on the edges will average out and move towards each other, snapping or sewing the edges together.

3. You can then use the **Smooth** tool in the paint geometry window to flatten everything a bit, and then touch up the blending areas with the **Paint Alpha** tool.

When multiple displacement surfaces are selected, the tools and area of influence will span the surfaces and affect every selected face. Select both the displacements, and you can smooth them both at the same time.

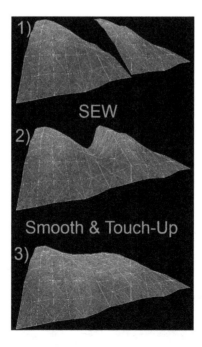

In order to properly sew the two displacements together, their object edges need to be touching. If one vertex isn't touching the other, the displacements will not sew. It might be counterintuitive at first, but it is important to remember that the displacement surface does not dictate the sewing action. In the following image, note that the displacement surface aligns nicely to the neighboring displacement. They will not sew together because the brush edges are not aligned.

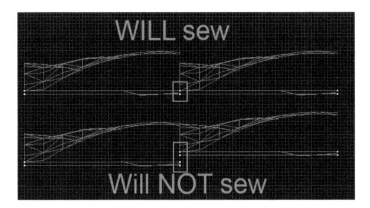

When using the **Paint Geometry** tool to manipulate multiple displacement surfaces, make sure to enable **auto-sew** to ensure that all edges stay together.

Subdividing

If you have two displacement surfaces that meet at a right angle, smoothing the corner manually can be a hassle and will be nearly impossible to get it perfect. Thankfully, Hammer has a **Subdivide** feature that will automatically smoothen the transitions between two or more displacement edges. Like the sew function, subdivisions will only work properly if the edges of the two surfaces are aligned with each other.

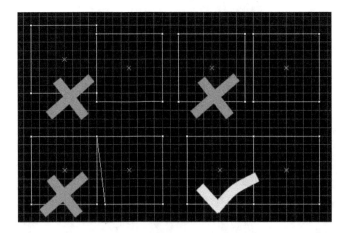

To see the power of the subdivision function, create a cube of any size with any texture, create power of three displacements on all sides, and then press the **Subdivide** button. You have now just turned a cube into a sphere! While the subdivision result isn't perfectly spherical, you can see how powerful this function is.

Creating caves quickly

The subdivide function can also be used to quickly make caves. Create a hallway and displace only the surfaces on the inside. Subdivide the whole thing (this might take a moment) and marvel at the results!

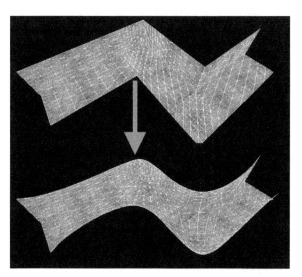

After subdividing, you will probably want to modify the displacement some more to add in some details. Open up the **Paint Geometry** tool and change the **Axis** to **face normal**. Click on **AutoSew** to automatically sew any seams and modify the radius to an acceptable value. When the **face normal** mode is selected, it defaults to modifying the displacement surface on the Z axis. We can change the axis orientation to any combination of X, Y, and Z by *Alt* + right-clicking on a displacement face. While holding *Shift*, you can now control the height or depth of any angle you like.

Sculpting

If you would like to make larger outdoor areas, it's a bit easier to use the **sculpting tool**. It has almost the same functionality as the paint geometry tool, but it's more suited for long, flowing strokes of mesh deformation.

Create a flat, square, grass-textured brush about 512 units long and 512 units wide; the height doesn't matter. Copy the brush five times to make a 2 x 3 grid of grass brushes, and then create power 3 displacements on the top faces of the six brushes. Click on the **Sculpt** button on the **Displacement** tab to open the sculpt menu.

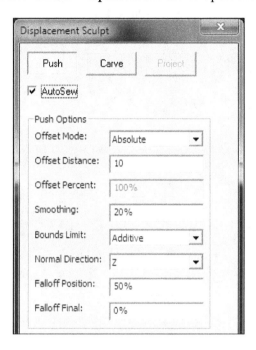

There are two usable modes in the **Sculpt** tool. The first is the **Push** mode. There are two push modes: **Absolute** and **Adaptive**. Absolute mode will raise or lower the mesh by the offset distance. You can control the amount of **Smoothing** and **Falloff** parameters as well. The **Bounds Limit** field can be **Additive** or **Attenuated**. If **Attenuated** is selected, the offset will not go any further than the offset distance from the previous location. For example, if a mesh point is at a vertical position of 20 units, and your offset distance is 10, the point will not reach higher than 30 units if pulled, and won't dip below 10 units if pushed.

It's a good idea to start small with the sculpt tool, so set the **Offset Distance** field to 2 units with **Offset Mode**, **Bounds Limit**, and **Normal Direction** set to `Absolute`, `Additive`, and `Z`, respectively.

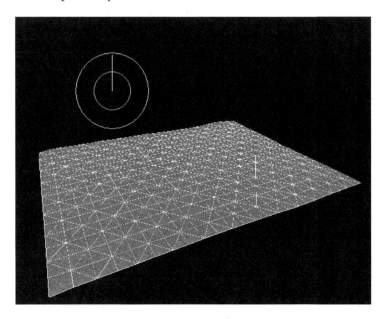

Your cursor will be shown as two concentric circles with a white line stemming from the center. The white line shows the direction of the deformation, the outer green circle shows the final falloff position, and the inner circle shows the start of the falloff.

Left-clicking will raise the mesh in the direction of the white line, whereas holding *Ctrl* while left-clicking will push the mesh in the opposite direction. Holding *Shift* while left-clicking will smoothen the mesh by the specified smoothing percentage, and you can change the size of the sculpting brush by right-clicking and dragging the mouse to the left to shrink and right to grow.

The cursor will always affect the same screen area; so, if you're zoomed out, you will affect a larger area than you will if you are zoomed in. This makes it easy to zoom in on small details but keep the same brush size.

The **Adaptive** sculpt mode uses the percent scale and can be very sensitive. It's a good idea to start with a percentage around 1-5 percent and then adjust it from there.

Carving

There is another very powerful terrain tool called the **Carve** tool. You can use it instead of the other tools or in addition to them.

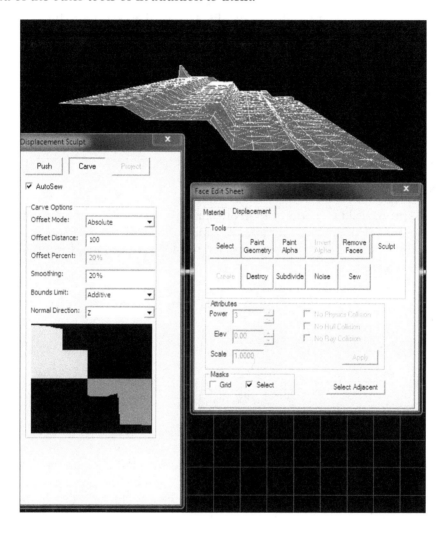

The **Carve** mode allows you to draw a displacement profile in the black box. The green portion will be raised up, while the red portion will be pushed in. The **Carve** tool works best when the displacement surface is viewed perpendicular to the surface normal. After drawing your profile, left-click and drag the cursor across the displacement surface to raise or lower the displacement according to the profile you have drawn; right-click to reverse the profile.

Creating props

Props help to decorate the world. They take less computer power to render and simulate than world geometry, but you need third-party software in order to create them. All props are point entities and are placed into the map with the entity tool.

Creating static props

Most of the props used in a Source map are static props. Static props account for any nonmoving (static) object. Light posts, wall clocks, trees, and pipes are all examples of items that can be static props. Let's place a tree on the dirt mound we have just created.

In the **Objects** drop-down, select prop_static and then left-click on the dirt mound in the 3D window to place a prop_static entity. It will be displayed as a red box. Left-click on it twice or hit *Alt + Enter* to bring up the object properties. In order to define which model we want to use for the prop, select the **World model** property, and click on **browse** to bring up the **Model Browser** window.

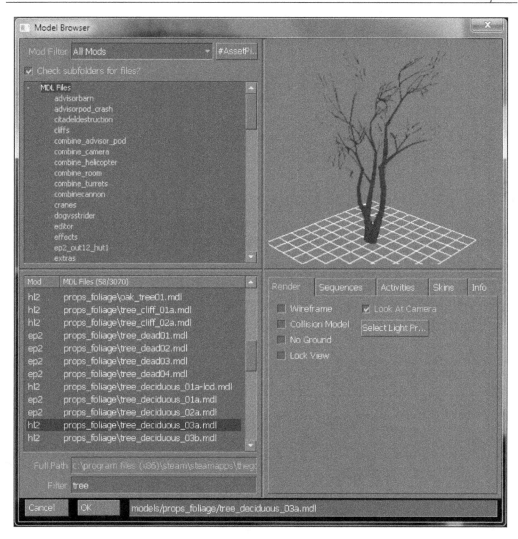

The model browser allows you to filter and search for all the models you can place in a map. Below the 3D preview, there are five tabs that give you more information about the model. The **Render** tab allows you to view different features of the model such as the wireframe view and collision mesh. The **Sequences** tab lists all the animations for the model, while the **Activities** tab lists some special model functions that make use of the animations. Each model has at least one **Skin** attributed to it that defines which textures it uses, and the **Info** tab will list some special properties of the model and tell you if it can be a static, physics, or a dynamic prop.

Type `tree` into the **Filter** to search for all the available tree models, and select **models/props_foliage/tree_deciduous_03a.mdl**. Check the **Info** tab to make sure that the **Static** tab is checked, which means this model can be used as a static prop. Click on **Ok** to close the browser and return to the **prop_static** properties window. The only thing left to do now is to fine-tune the entity placement and make sure the tree is intersecting with the displacement.

Static props greatly increase the look and feel of your maps, but they don't move. If we want some props we can interact with, we need a **physics prop**.

Creating physics props

Physics props take advantage of the Source's physics engine. They interact with the player, world geometry, and other models, and have the ability to break apart into pieces known as **gibs**. Physics props are placed into the world just like static props are, but they use the **prop_physics** point entity. Let's place a breakable chair into the map to see what the physics engine can do. Place a **prop_physics** entity on the floor inside the house; open its properties and then the model browser via the world model property. Select the **models/props_c17/furniturechair001a.mdl** model and look at the **Info** tab in the **Model Browser** window. Note that the **physics** and **staticstatic** boxes are checked. This means that this model can act as a static prop or a physics prop. If the physics prop box was not checked, the compiler will report that as an error, and the model will not appear when you go to view it in the game.

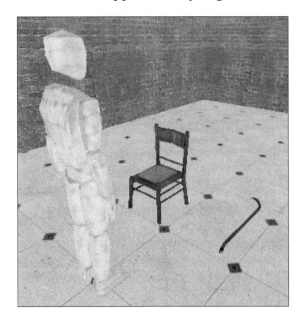

Place a **weapon_crowbar** point entity on the ground next to the chair so that we can test the `gib` functionality in the game. Compile the map, load it up, and see how the chair reacts to physics, collisions, and damage.

Creating dynamic props

Dynamic props, like the name suggests, have the ability to move. They do not move in reaction to physics inputs; rather, their animations are controlled with triggers. They are placed in the map just like a static or physics prop, the only difference being the entity they are created with, which is **prop_dynamic**. You will learn more about controlling these props in *Chapter 7, Triggers and the Input/Output System*, when you get more acquainted with the Input/Output system, but for now, just know that they exist!

Summary

There was a lot covered in this chapter. By now, you know the ins and outs of the Texture Application Tool. You can save a lot of time by utilizing the align buttons, and making a terrain is easy with the flexible displacement tool. Decals and overlays can help break up a stretch of repetitive textures, and since models are simple for the engine to render, you can pepper a map with detail without stressing the game engine!

Get your creative juices flowing because importing custom content is next!

5
Importing Custom Content

The Source SDK tools give access to hundreds of different models, sounds, and materials. *Half-Life 2* is based on a post-war, apocalyptic environment, and most of the materials include some wear, grunge, and destruction. If your mod does not follow this theme, you'll probably want to add some of your own content in the maps.

In this chapter, we will be learning the following topics:

- Creating materials
- Importing materials
- Importing models
- Importing sounds

Let's jump in!

Creating materials

Source materials are made up of two files:

- A **VTF (Valve Texture Format)** file that actually contains the image of how the VTF is rendered in-game
- A **VMT (Valve Material Type)** text-based file that defines the material type

You can have multiple VMT files that reference the same VTF file. So, you can have multiple materials that use the same image differently.

The .bin folder contains the program you need to create your own materials. All you need is an image editor capable of creating targa (.tga) files and a proper folder structure.

Setup

First, let's set up our folders. For `vtex.exe`, the texture-creating program, to function properly, you need to create two folders: one to hold the texture source files and another to hold the compiled materials. The first folder we need to create in your mod folder will hold all the TGA files. In this example, the `mytextures` folder will contain all of our textures. Create the following folders in your Steam folder as follows:

`steamapps\common\<your mod>\materialsrc\mytextures.`

Since I'm working with *Half-Life 2: Episode Two*, my folder location is `steamapps\common\Half-Life 2\ep2\materialsrc\mytextures`. It might be a good idea to create a shortcut to this folder in some place that is easily accessible, because this folder is located deep within the Steam folder.

Vtex needs to know where to put the converted texture files. Create another `mytextures` folder in the `materials` folder in the `ep2` folder. Again, since I am using *Half-Life 2: Episode Two*, I have created the following folder:

`steamapps\common\Half-Life 2\ep2\materials\mytextures`

This folder will contain the VMT and VTF files that Source will actually display in Hammer and in-game.

 All custom textures must be within a subfolder of the `materials` folder or else the game will not detect them.

The program used to create the textures is called `vtex.exe`, and it's located in the `.bin` folder. Again, following my *Half-Life 2: Episode Two* example, `vtex.exe` will be available at `Steam\steamapps\common\Half-Life 2\bin`. In order to make our lives a bit easier, create a shortcut to `vtex.exe` in the `materialsrc\mytextures` folder.

Creating a VTF file

Phew! that was exhausting. Now that we have set up our folders, we can get to the fun part—creating materials! All texture files that are created with Vtex need to be targa files and should have dimensions in factors of 2. Height and width values of 2, 4, 8, 16, 32, 64, 128, 256, 512, 1024, 2048, and so on, are all acceptable, but the default texture size is 512 x 512 so, that should be a great place to start. Once your targa file is created and saved in the proper folder (`materialsrc\mytextures`), drag the targa file onto the `vtex.exe` shortcut you previously created to create a VTF.

I have included a sample targa file called `texture01` for you to play around with, as shown in the following screenshot:

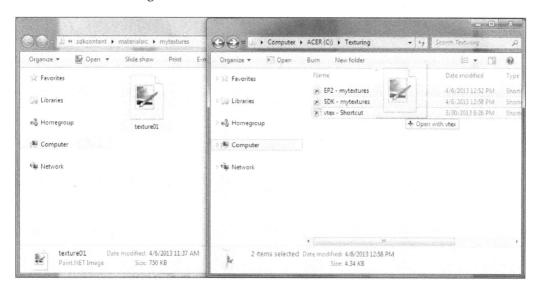

A command prompt window will appear showing you the input path, output path, and status of the file conversion as follows:

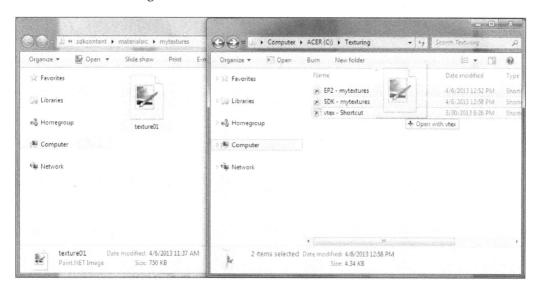

If everything is set up properly, you will see a newly created VTF file in the `mytextures` folder of your game directory.

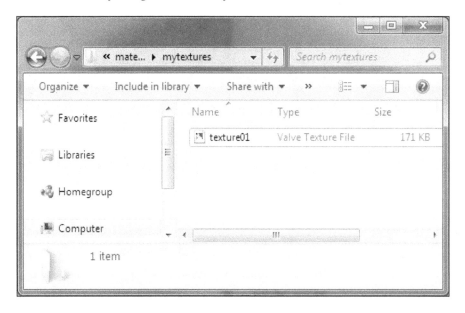

Creating a VMT file

Unfortunately, our VTF file is useless by itself. For the engine to recognize that file as a material, we need to create a VMT file that defines properties such as the render mode and material type. VTF files are just text files that are saved in the `.vmt` format. You can use any simple text editor, such as Notepad, to create them. Open Notepad and type the following code:

```
"LightmappedGeneric"
{
  "$basetexture" "mytextures/texture01"
  "$surfaceprop" "wood"
}
```

Let me explain how this all works.

- `Lightmappedgeneric`: This defines the texture as a normal light mapped texture. It can receive light information in game; most material files will begin with this.

- `$basetexture`: This defines the main VTF to display. The `mytextures/texture01` folder is the location of the VTF relative to the main materials folder.

- `$surfaceprop`: This tells the engine the type of surface material. When you damage this texture in-game, it will create sounds and damage decals based on the surface properties. In my example, this material is wood, but there are dozens of other choices. A full list of valid surface properties can be found on Valve's wiki at `https://developer.valvesoftware.com/wiki/Material_surface_properties`.

Save the file as `texture01.vmt` to complete the material creation. When you browse for your texture in Hammer, you will be searching for the VMT file and not the VTF file.

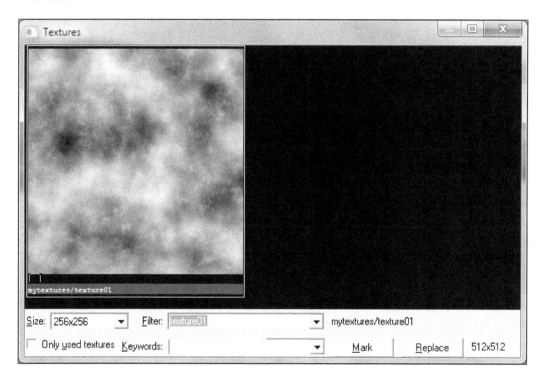

When you run the map in-game, you'll notice that the decals and sounds that are produced when the surface is damaged match those of the surface properties. In this example, the material is wood.

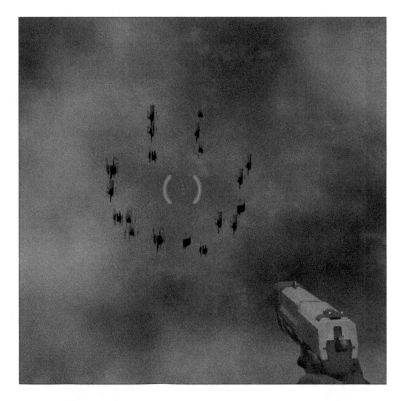

Using VTFEdit

There's an easier way to create materials. VTFEdit is a tool created by Nem (Ryan Greggs) that puts an easy-to-use GUI over the default SDK texture creation. You can grab it from `http://nemesis.thewavelength.net/index.php?c=238#p238`. You'll need Microsoft's .NET framework to run the program (also available at the previous web page) as well.

Using VTFEdit is much easier than typing your own commands and creating a folder network. Run VTFEdit and navigate to **File** | **Import** to choose an image to import.

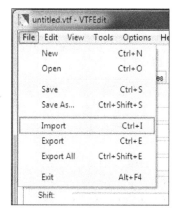

A great thing about VTFEdit is its ability to import multiple image types. As long as you conform to the size constraints, you can import bitmaps, PNGs, JPEGs, and many more. After choosing your file, you will see a prompt showing a slew of options. Click on **OK** to continue, as shown in the following screenshot, since the defaults will most likely suit your needs:

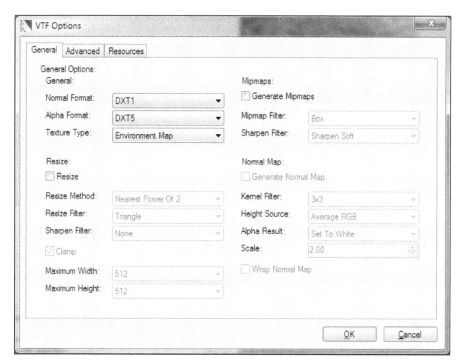

Once you have imported an image, navigate to **File | Save** to create a VTF based on your imported image, making sure you choose the mod/materials/mytextures folder. Wasn't that so much easier than before?

Now, we need to create the VMT text file. VTFEdit makes our lives easier once again. Instead of coding our own file, the program does it for us! To see how easy this is, navigate to **Tools | Create VMT File**:

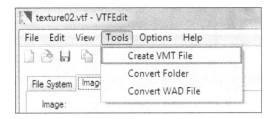

We will be greeted with a window that will let us choose which VTF we want to create the material with. By default, the VTF we have just created will be at the top of our list.

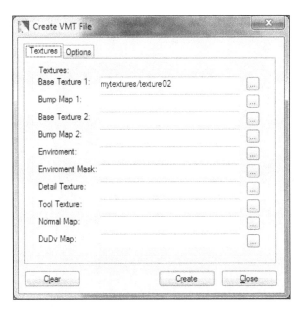

Have a look at the preceding screenshot. The **Base Texture 1** field will be filled in with the texture you have just created. In my example, this is `mytextures/texture02`. If you have a bump map created for your texture, you can add it to this material by clicking on the ellipsis (...) next to the **Bump Map 1** field. Since this texture is a simple brick wall, we don't need a bump map. Let's move on to the **Options** tab to see some other options.

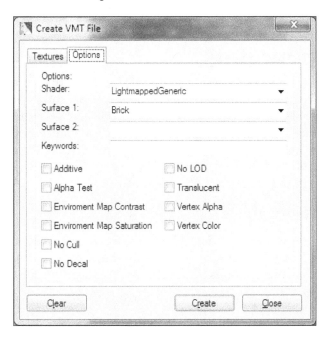

The **Options** tab gives us more control over the texture. This is where you can select the surface properties and some other special texture attributes. Again, instead of typing the code, VTFEdit makes our lives easier by allowing us to simply tick checkboxes to choose options. Since we are using a brick texture, select **Brick** for **Surface 1**. If you're not using a brick-like texture, select whichever material is closest; there are many to choose from. This is a standard texture, so we're not going to need any other special options here. Click on **Create** to continue and bring up a save prompt. Name your VMT something along the lines of `brick01` or `mytexture02` and save it in your `mytextures` folder.

That's it, you're done! You will now be able to see your texture in the texture browser within Hammer and in the game.

Importing other materials

If you want to import premade materials into your game, just place the VMT and VTF files into any subfolder within the `materials` folder of your game folder. The materials need to be in their own folder. It's also easy to keep them organized if they are in folders, because you can search for specific folders while using the texture browser in Hammer.

Importing models

Models need to be created and textured with third-party software, but the materials and models still need to go into the proper folders in order to be displayed in the game. If you have a model called `mymodel.mdl`, this model needs to be placed into its own folder within a subfolder of the `models` folder of your game. Wait, what? It's a common practice for each custom model to be placed within its own folder. If you had a box model called `mybox.mdl`, it would be in a folder called `mybox` within the `mymodels` folder within the `models` folder. For example:

```
Steam\SteamApps\common\Half-Life 2\ep2\models\mymodels\mybox\
```

The materials for your custom models go into the `materials` folder in a similar manner. The same folder structure exists beneath the `models` folder and the `materials` folder, yet one contains the `.mdl` files and the other contains the `.vmf` and `.vmt` files.

```
Steam\SteamApps\common\Half-Life 2\ep2\materials\models\mymodels\mybox
```

The folders get nested pretty deep and it can be pretty confusing at first glance, but everything is neatly organized. You will know that everything worked properly when you open the model browser and your model is there. If you can't see your model, it was compiled incorrectly or the pieces are in the wrong locations. Double-check everything!

Importing sounds

Just like models and textures, sounds require their own folder within the `sound` folder:

```
C:\Program Files\Steam\steamapps\username\half-life 2 episode 2\ep2\
sound
```

The source engine supports both MP3 and WAV files. Any `.mp3` file can be placed in the `sound` folder, and this will be recognized by Source and played in-game. However, WAV files are a bit trickier. The highest quality WAV file that Source will play is PCM 16-bit WAV at 44 KHz (refer to `https://developer.valvesoftware.com/wiki/`).

Click on the **Refresh** sounds button in the sound browser within Hammer to reload the new sounds so that they can be previewed. WAV files are the only files that can be previewed.

Summary

Creating textures is pretty easy once the proper folder structure is set up, and importing custom content is as simple as placing the proper files into the correct folders. Sounds go in the `sound` folder, models go in the `models` folder, and materials go into the `materials` folder. Custom models are created in third-party modeling applications such as Blender, 3DSMAX, or Maya. Prepare to bring some light into your world because next up is lighting!

6

Lighting and Compiling

Welcome to the world of lighting and compiling! It's generally accepted that lighting can make or break a map, and this chapter will show you how to avoid some common pitfalls while utilizing some of Source's most advanced lighting features to make your environment shine.

This chapter will cover the following topics:

- Using lights
- Emphasizing lights
- Modifying the Lightmap Grid
- Assigning Smoothing groups
- Compiling concepts
- Placing cubemaps
- Adding color correction

The best way to learn is to jump in, so let's get started!

Using lights

There are a multitude of different types of lights available in Source. Learning how to use each type of light is very important in setting the mood in your maps. Every type of light entity has its own special properties that help define the look and feel of the map's lighting. However, most light entities have a common brightness parameter that controls not only the brightness but also the color.

The **Brightness** parameter contains four three-digit numbers separated by a space. The first three numbers specify the color in **Red**, **Green**, and **Blue** (**RGB**) format, while the last number specifies the light brightness. The default brightness is 255 255 255 200, which is a white light with a brightness of 200. Hammer has a built-in color picker, so you don't have to mess around with the raw RGB numbers, although it makes copying and pasting colors from outside applications easy. There is no specific unit for the brightness number. Higher values are brighter, whereas lower values are dimmer. Let's take a look at a specific light entities.

Using point lights

Point lights are the simplest of all lights available in the Source engine. Point lights emit light in all directions from a single point in space. You can think of a point light as a standard light bulb. However, instead of emitting light from a filament inside a glass bulb, the light comes from the direct center—just a single, invisible point in space. You cannot see where the light is coming from, just that there is light being cast in all directions.

The entity that point lights are created from is simply called light. We have used these before but we just skimmed the surface.

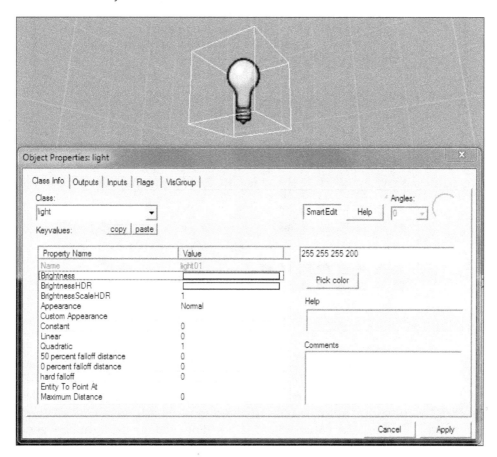

Have a look at the preceding screenshot. You will see a number of different parameters for **light** that are explained as follows:

- **Name:** This parameter gives your light a name if you would like to turn the light on and off. Lights will work fine without names, and they are set to the on state by default; however, you won't be able to turn them off.

- **Brightness:** This parameter controls the color of the light. When you click on the **Pick color** button, a color picker will appear, which will automatically fill in the RGB (Red, Green, and Blue) values when you have chosen the color you want.

Different light colors have implied moods

A warm white/yellow light is familiar and safe, while blue lights can make an area feel cold and uninviting. Think about which mood you would like to imply in a given area while choosing your light colors!

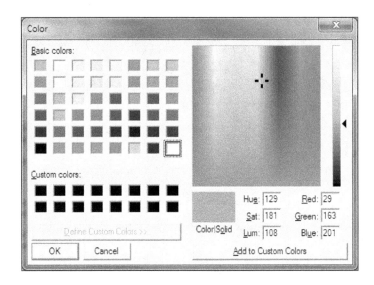

- **BrightnessHDR**: This setting will control the brightness of the light when the map is compiled with HDR. This parameter is set just like the regular brightness setting but will override the standard brightness when compiled in the HDR mode. A value of -1 -1 -1 1 will not change the light between modes and is set as default.

- **BrightnessScaleHDR:** This parameter scales the brightness when in the HDR mode to give the effect of increased or decreased light. A value of 1 (set as default) will not change the default brightness.

- **Appearance**: This parameter controls the dynamic brightness of your light. There are different presets you can choose from, such as **fluorescent flicker** or **candle** effects. The default is **none** and that should work just fine for most situations.

- **Custom Appearance**: This parameter allows you to enter a custom appearance for the light in the form of a string. You can enter the letters a-z in a long sequence with the letter **a** representing 100 percent of brightness and **z** representing zero percent brightness. Each letter in the string changes the brightness for one-tenth of a second.

- **Constant**: Set this parameter to 1 to force the light to have a constant brightness along the reach of the light.

- **Linear**: Set this parameter to 1 to force the light to have a linear falloff. The brightness decreases linearly with respect to the distance away from the light origin. The light is 1/64 times the brightness of the origin, which is 64 units away from the light.

- **Quadratic**: Set this parameter to 1 (default) to force the light to have a quadratic falloff. The brightness decrease is equal to the square of the distance away from the light origin. If you're 64 units away from the light, the brightness is 1/4096 (64*64) of the original. Unless you want some special lighting, keep this setting.

- **50 percent falloff distance**: This parameter sets the distance you want to one half of the light's brightness.

- **0 percent falloff distance**: This parameter sets the distance you want to 1/256th of the light's brightness.

- **Hard Falloff**: This parameter forces the 0 percent falloff distance to have 0 percent light.

- **Entity to Point At**: This parameter has no effect on point lights.

- **Maximum Distance**: This parameter has no effect on point lights.

The following image gives some examples of the different light styles that all have the same brightness. Check out the CH6_falloff example map for even more examples.

Using spot lights

Spot lights emit light from a central point, but their light emission is focused in a single direction controlled by two cones. There is a bright inner cone and a fading outer cone that control the angle of reach and the focus of the light. Spot lights are useful for ceiling lights, light posts, desk lamps, or any light source that will cast light in a specific direction.

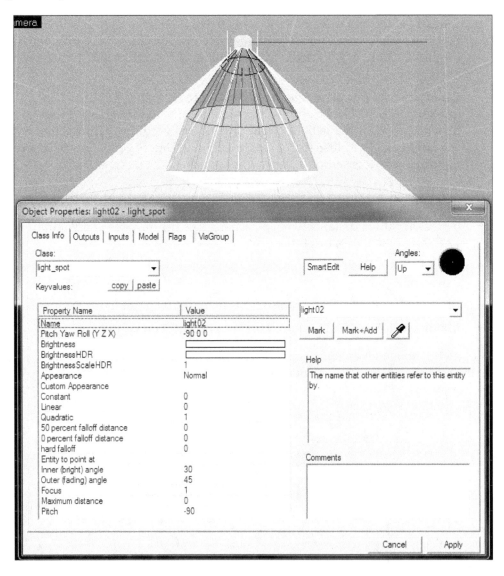

The properties of **light_spot** are very similar to the standard **light**; the only difference is an addition of **Outer (fading) angle** and **Inner (bright) angle**. Changing these angles allow you to control the width and brightness of the light. As you can see from the preceding image, the light is cast downward only because the **pitch**, or vertical angle, is set to **-90**. A value of **0** or **180** will cast light horizontally, while **90** or **-90** will cast light vertically. There is no light emission outside the cone, so spotlights are often combined with dull point lights to convey a more realistic light emission around the source of the **light_spot** entity.

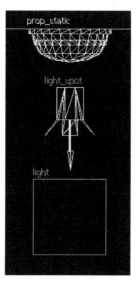

In-game, you'll be able to see the effectiveness of the combination of **light_spot** and **light** as shown in the preceding image. The following image shows the effect of combining spot lights and point lights:

Using light environments

The **light_env** emits light from the **skybox** texture. The **brightness** and **angles** are set just like a **light_spot** entity but there are no cone angles to specify. Light will always be cast at the same angle unless **sun spread angle** is specified to break up the light direction, as shown in the following screenshot:

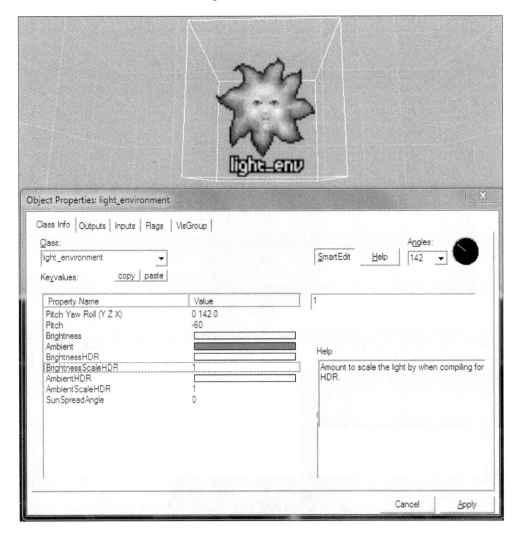

Brightness and **BrightnessHDR** are set like normal lights but there is also an **ambient** setting that defines the brightness of the darker areas of the map. Wherever a shadow is cast, the ambient light will be applied in that area.

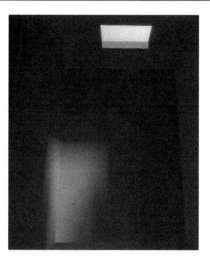

Using dynamic lights

Dynamic lights and **light_dynamic** act similar to spot lights, but they are calculated in real time. The word dynamic means changing; dynamic lights can change color, brightness, and angle and can be used in a variety of situations. For example, you can parent a **light_dynamic** to a hanging light, and when shot, the light will move around with the swinging fixture. However, you should use dynamic lights sparingly in your maps because they take a lot of processing power to display due to the real-time light calculations.

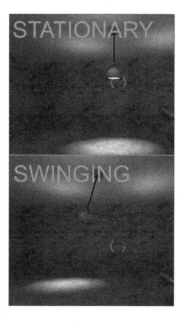

You'll notice that the parameters are nearly the same as the **light_spot** entity. There are some key differences, however. The **inner (bright) angle** and **outer (fading) angle** parameters only affect models such as props, NPCs, and your weapon. The **spotlight end radius** entity affects how the world (brushes and displacements) is lit by making a circle of light on the ground with that radius. The **Brightness** parameter is not tied into the **color** setting like other lights, and it doesn't follow the same scale either. A **brightness** value of **5** is a good place to start with a **light_dynamic** entity. The **Brightness** parameter also doesn't affect how far the light is cast either; this is directly controlled with the **maximum distance** parameter, which needs to be set equal to or greater than the surfaces or models you want to light.

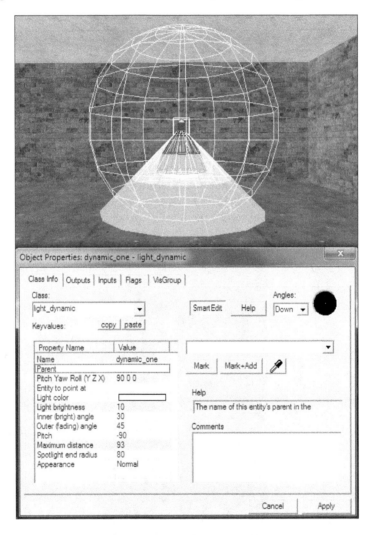

Using texture lights

There's a way to light your map without the need of entities! **Texture lights** emit light from the surface of a material. The color and brightness of the emitted light are specified within the `lights.rad` file, which is located in your game folder. In the texture browser, you can't tell if a material will emit light, so you should check the `lights.rad` file before you compile.

The `lights.rad` file is a simple text file that is saved with a `.rad` extension. All it contains is a list of texture names and their associated brightness values with each texture residing on a separate line. For example, I want the **metal/metalwall013a** texture to emit a reddish-brown light with a brightness of **1500**. My `lights.rad` file would look like the following:

```
metal/metalwall013a 153 69 13 1500
```

Simple enough, right? Now just save it in the `base` game folder. So, since I'm using *Half-Life 2: Episode Two*, I will save it at `Steam\SteamApps\common\Half-Life 2`. Make sure to select **All Files** next to the **Save as Type** description so it will save as a `.rad` file and not a `.txt` file.

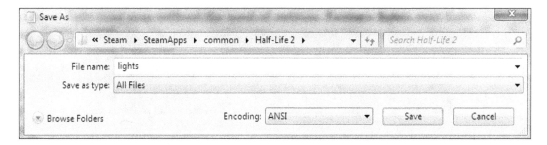

When I compile my map, the log will show that it is using a texture from the `lights.rad` file by displaying **[Reading texlights from 'lights.rad'][1 texlights parsed from 'lights.rad']**. In-game, the texture will emit light from the surface! Texture lights tend to be pretty dull, so don't be afraid to crank your brightness values past 1500.

Texture lights are often used to emit light from light textures. Combining a texture light with a sprite (mentioned later in this chapter) provides a very convincing lighting effect.

Using projected textures

Projected textures are not exactly lights but they cast a colored texture in a specific direction similar to **light_spot**, but instead of a cone-shaped emission, the project texture had a pyramid-shaped emission. Projected textures have the unique ability to cast shadows through alpha channels in textures. They're very useful for giving a dramatic back-lit effect through a grate or fence, but like dynamic lights, they take a lot of processing power to display.

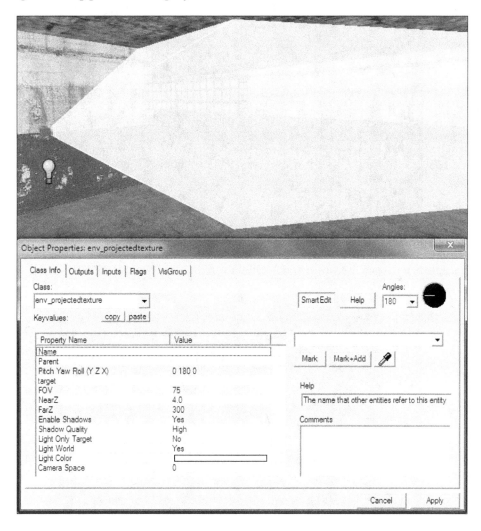

The entity used is **env_projectedtexture**, and the light color is set just like the **Brightness** parameter in any other light. However, **Shadows** have to be enabled manually. In this example, this projected texture is shining through a grate across a hallway. **Shadows** are enabled and the light color is left at the default white with a brightness value of 200. There is a dull point light in the nook with the projected texture just to give the illusion that there is light coming from behind the grate. I also placed the same grate with just a point light inside to show the difference in effect.

The **light** entity casts a standard light cone out from the inset in the hallway.

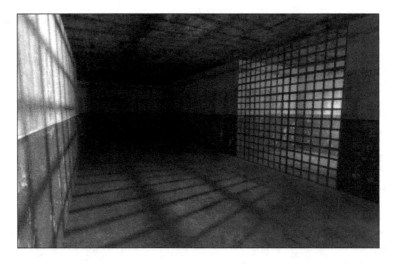

The **env_projectedtexture** entity casts shadows created with the texture's alpha channel.

Projected textures will also cast shadows of NPCs and models, but they will not cast shadows of the player because there is no player model in Half-Life 2.

 Only one projected texture can be rendered at any time. Keep this in mind because your flashlight counts as a projected texture and render errors will occur if you use both simultaneously!

Emphasizing lights

We all know that light doesn't radiate without a source. Lights in your map should have a place of origin. Thankfully, there's a collection of models available to use as light sources. Let's start with a simple point light source.

Placing point light sources

This is a concrete hallway with a simple point light in the middle of it. The light comes from nowhere, and the overall effect is boring and unrealistic. Let's put some light fixtures in the hallway to add some realism.

Add a **prop_static** entity using the **light_cagelight02_on.mdl** model to the map, and align it to the wall, as shown in the following image. Make sure to choose the correct **skin** entity for the light, as some light models can have an on skin and an off skin. Move the **light** entity a few units out in front of the model and reduce the **brightness** parameter to **80**.

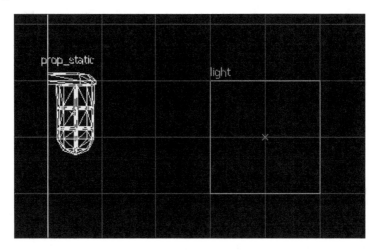

Give the map a quick test-compile to check the results. If the lighting on the model is looking a bit off, set the **disable shadows** property in the **prop_static** entity to **yes** to clean up the results.

Even though the map is darker, and the lighting isn't perfect, you still get the idea that the light is being emitted from the cage light model mounted on the wall.

We can even add a bit more realism by using a glowing effect that will fade as the player approaches the light. Place an **env_sprite** point entity inside the light model. In this case, the only two parameters we need to change are the **render mode** parameter and the **Size of Glow Proxy Geometry** parameter. Change **render mode** to **glow** so that the sprite scales it relative to our position, and change the **Size of Glow Proxy Geometry** parameter to **5** to make sure the sprite will render properly when the origin is inside a model. Give the map another compile to check out your results.

Placing spot light sources

Spot lights can also use a model and glow effect to increase their realism. A fluorescent light model can benefit from an entity called **env_lightglow**. The **env_lightglow** entity allows you to specify the width and height of a glow effect as well as the distances they start to fade at. The settings are set just like a regular **sprite** entity.

Modifying Lightmap Grid

Lightmap Grid controls the level of shadow detail on any brush face. By default, the Lightmap Grid size is **16**, which means lighting is calculated every 16 units on a specific brush face. By decreasing the size of Lightmap Grid, you can get sharper shadows at the expense of compile time and memory. Increasing Lightmap Grid removes the shadow detail, but it will speed up your compile time and decrease the size of the compiled map. Let's learn more about these useful settings.

In order to see Lightmap Grid on your brush faces, left-click on the top-left corner of the 3D view and select **3D Lightmap Grid**, as shown in the following screenshot:

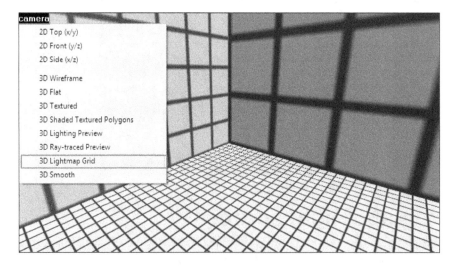

Once you select this **View** mode, you will see a grid on each brush instead of a texture or flat color. As previously mentioned, the default Lightmap Grid size is **16** units. This default color scheme is a dark blue grid overlaid on top of a solid, light-blue background. If the grid size is below **16** units, the background color changes to yellow indicating that the face contains a higher than normal Lightmap Grid density. If the grid size is above **16** units, the background changes to a darker blue indicating that the face contains a lower than normal Lightmap Grid density.

The Lightmap Grid scale property is located in the top-right corner of **Texture Application Tool**.

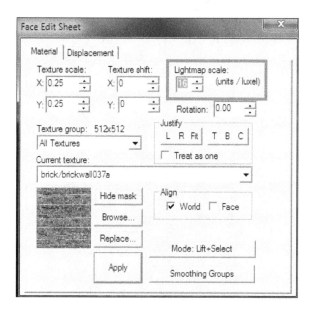

To make a Lightmap scale change, select a brush face, change the **Lightmap scale** value, and click on **Apply**. In the following figure, you can see how drastic the effect Lightmap Grid size has on your map's shadows. The smaller the Lightmap Grid size, the sharper your shadows will be. If you want to accent the shadows in a particular area, shrink Lightmap Grid before you try anything else!

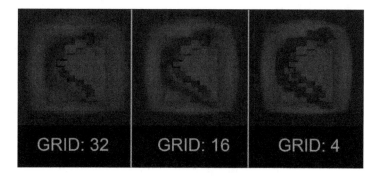

Assigning Smoothing groups

Smoothing groups are used to smoothen the transition between faces on curved brushes. In order to apply a smoothing group to a brush, you first need to open **Texture Application Tool** and click on the **Smoothing Groups** button located in the bottom-right corner. A dialog box will open displaying 24 **Smooth** group buttons and eight **Hard** group buttons, as shown in the following screenshot:

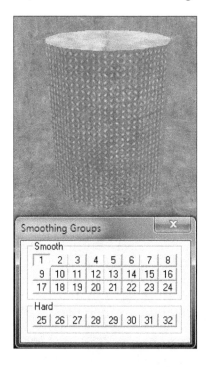

Select the desired faces to be smoothed and click on a **Smooth** number button to assign those faces a smoothing group. Shadows cast on the object will be blended around the brush faces based on the density of the face Lightmap Grid. Like before, the smaller the Lightmap Grid size, the more lighting detail the brush contains, and the smoother the transition between the faces will be. However, keep in mind that Lightmap Grid needs to be equal to or smaller than the width of the brush face in order to smoothen it properly. So, if you have a brush face that is **16** units wide, your Lightmap Grid can be a maximum of **16** units to achieve any smoothing effect.

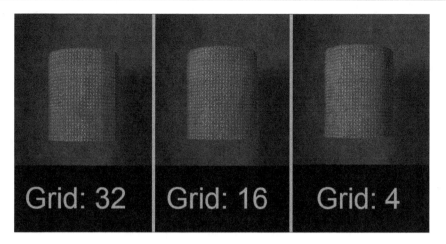

You can see that the transitions between faces on rounded surfaces get smoother when you assign smoothing groups and decrease the Lightmap Grid size! Use this to your advantage when placing pillars, columns, and rounded corners in your maps!

In the CH6_smoothing example map, you can see that each of the individual cylinders have the same smoothing group assigned to them. Since the faces between cylinders do not touch each other, it's fine to leave them as the same smoothing group. Make sure to only use one smoothing group on any specific group of touching brushes. Faces can also be assigned more than one smoothing group to blend multiple brush faces together.

 You can force objects to have a hard shadow between them by assigning a **Hard** group number instead of a **Smooth** group number.

Compiling concepts

Up until now, we have just been doing normal compiles during our tests, and we haven't really paid much attention to any of the advanced features or what each specific option controls. Doing normal compiles is just fine for testing, but let's explore the different stages of the compile process and how to tweak the settings to our liking.

Checking for problems

Before you even think about compiling a map, you should always check it for problems. In Hammer, press *Alt + P* to check the map for problems. If you're neat, organized, or just plain lucky, you will not have any problems, and a happy dialog box will appear as follows:

If you don't have any errors, great! You can go ahead and compile. However, if you do have errors, you will see a list of everything that's wrong in your map, as shown in the following screenshot:

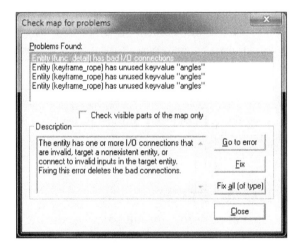

A few common errors and their solutions are:

- Invalid solid structure
  - Solution: Concave or other type of brush. Click on **Fix** to resolve or recreate the object.

- There is no player start
  - Solution: Add an **info_player_start** entity.

- Entity (entity_type) has unused keyvalue "angles"
  - ° Solution: Always appears with some entities. It can usually be ignored, but the **Fix** button will resolve it.

- Entity (entity_type) has bad I/O connections
  - ° Solution: There is a bad reference in an I/O connection. Fixing it will delete the I/O reference.

Most of the time, the **Fix** button will resolve the error. If it doesn't, you can check the VDC website at `https://developer.valvesoftware.com/wiki/Compile_Errors`, and do a web search, or check a mapping community website such as `twhl.info`. Someone must have probably run into the same problem before, and most people would be glad to help you resolve it.

After checking your map for problems, press *F9* to bring up the **Run Map** dialog box as follows:

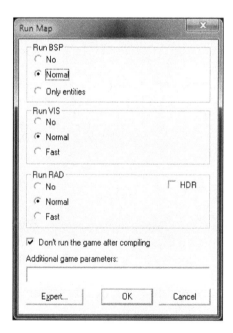

Running BSP

Without going into too much detail, the **Binary Space Partition** (**BSP**) part of the compile process takes all the world brushes, displacements, and models, and creates a playable `.bsp` (map) file with them. It is this process that actually creates the world out of the `.vmf` (map) file that you create with Hammer.

Other than the **Normal** option, there are two other selections for **BSP: No** and **Only entities**, as shown in the following screenshot:

No will not run the BSP program meaning that all changes to your brushwork or displacements will not be updated when you compile. In order for your map to function properly, a previous compilation using BSP must have been made. The **VIS** and **RAD** programs will still run with BSP disabled, so this can shave off a few seconds your compile time if you want to just do a lighting check.

Only entities will update the location and function of any brush-based entities that were changed after the last compile. This setting is useful when used in conjunction with disabling VIS and RAD to check complex entity setups and scripts.

Running VIS

VIS tells the game engine which parts of your map are visible from any other point. The following screenshot shows the VIS portion of the compile prompt:

It does this by slicing empty space into areas known as **visleafs**. Without diving too deep into the actual function of a visleaf, just know that any object's visibility is controlled by the visleaf it occupies and any surrounding neighbors. If you can see a visleaf, everything inside it and any of its neighbors is rendered. VIS will create one or more visleafs between each brush, and it mostly prefers cubic shapes over angled geometry. In general, the lesser visleafs, the better.

To see the visleafs created during the compile process, navigate to **Map | Load Portal File** after you have compiled one of your maps.

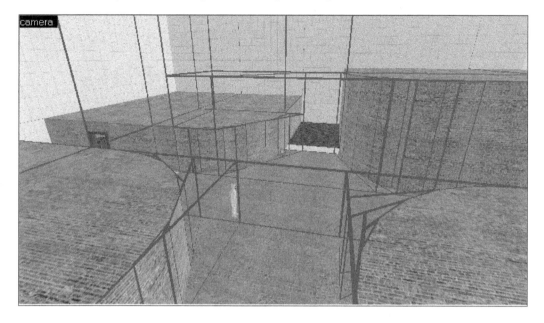

Angled world brushes cut square visleafs into wedge pieces, which can drastically increase the amount of visleafs in a map. The lesser the visleafs in a map, the faster the map compiles, and the faster it runs in-game. So, it's a good mapping practice to turn angled and complex geometry into **func_detail** entities because they do not cut visleafs!

 If your map is taking a while to compile, load the portal file and see if you can trim it down a bit.

Note the difference when the angled wall sections are turned into **func_detail** entities. Even in such a small, simple map, the percentage of leaves was reduced by around 27 percent (from 93 to 73)!

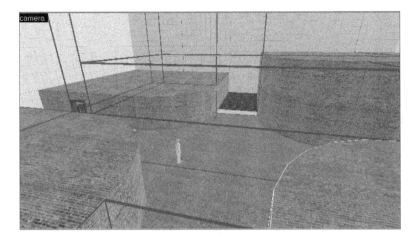

Don't go too crazy turning every piece of curved geometry into the **func_detail** entities; only world brushes seal the map from the void, and you may create a leak if you turn an exterior brush into **func_detail**!

If VIS is not calculated, the entire map will be visible at all times. If you have a beefy gaming rig, this won't be too much of a problem, but on larger maps, rendering everything at once will bring even the best machine to its knees. No map should ever be released or considered final without running VIS in the compile. Disabling VIS can be handy at times if you make good use of the cordon tool to limit your compile bounds, and you want to check out some entity setups.

RAD

RAD is short for radiosity, and it calculates lighting in your map. Each light source in the map gets analyzed to see how far the light is cast, and how many times the light bounces off each surface. Lights that turn on and off or have a flicker will have a separate RAD calculation for each brightness value. So, a light that can be turned on and off will have two RAD calculations, and a light that stays on all the time will have one RAD calculation. Lights, for example, that have a custom appearance of **aaahhhmmmzzzz**, will have four RAD calculations (one for each letter). So, if you're using a lot of flickering lights in your map, expect to wait a little bit for RAD to do its duty. The lighting calculations make up the majority of your compile time and will eat most of your computer's resources. If you're compiling a large or complex-lit map, it's best to leave your computer alone while the map compiles because it can take hours to complete.

If you try to multitask while compiling, you might freeze the process, and VIS or RAD might not respond. It's highly recommended to leave your computer alone while compiling a large map; especially, during a final compile. Take a nap, take a break, maybe get a cup of tea, and sit outside! Patience is the key.

If you disable RAD while compiling, your map will become what's known as **full bright**. There will be no lighting information in your map, and all the textures will be rendered at their native (100 percent bright) color.

 The sprite on the light fixture is still visible, but it isn't emitting any light.

Full bright maps are very unattractive, but compiling without RAD can save a lot of time even over fast compiles. Running a map without RAD is very useful for testing entity setups because you're cutting over 50 percent of your compile time out.

Fast RAD compiles are quicker than normal RAD compiles. They don't look pretty, but running with fast RAD during the bulk of the development process will save you hours in the long run. Usually, while creating maps, lighting is tweaked in the end or else normal RAD compiles will eat your precious time for no reason.

Compiling with HDR

HDR stands for **High Dynamic Range**. HDR makes a map's visuals more attractive by mimicking the way a human's eye reacts to differences in brightness. HDR makes bright lights whiter, dark corners blacker, and simulates the glow or bloom of light oversaturation. If you then walk between different areas of brightness, your view will take a few seconds to adjust to the new area. As we can see in the following image, compiling with HDR when it is enabled will nearly double your compile time, but it's well worth it for the added effect:

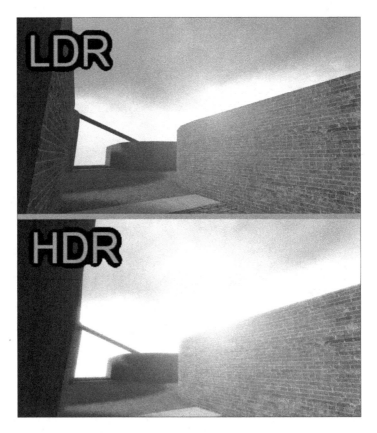

The Expert mode

You can turn on the expert compiling mode by clicking on the **Expert** button from the standard compiling menu.

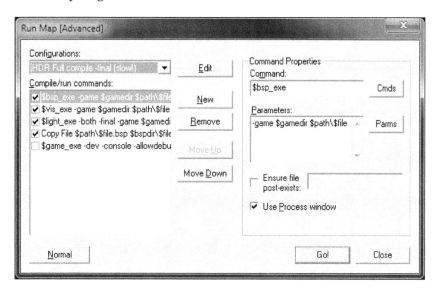

The expert mode allows you more control over the BSP, VIS, RAD, and other settings in your compile. When you enter the expert mode, you might be overwhelmed, but this just exposes the parameters that are passed to the individual compile programs. Have a look at the preceding screenshot. Source has a few precanned expert compile modes that are quite useful. The easiest way to do a final HDR compile is to pull down the **Configurations** selection box and select **HDR Full compile –final**. This will run BSP, VIS, and RAD at their maximum settings. This will take a very, very long time if your map is complex (a few hours). The results will be worth it though.

If you wish to modify any specific command parameters, select it from the **Compile/ run commands:** area, and add other compile parameters in the right-hand side. The most useful parameters are **-both** and **-final** for the RAD program. The **-both** parameter compiles LDR (regular lighting) and HDR. The **-final** parameter should be used on the last compile of the map to make the lighting look the best it can.

Checking for and fixing leaks

During the compile process, the map is also checked for leaks. If your map does not look correct in-game, or if it's taking a dreadfully long time to compile, you can check the compile log to see if you have a leak anywhere. An easy way to tell if your map has a leak is to look at water while you're in-game. You should be able to see right through it.

The compile log will be displayed at the end of a compile, but if you have closed it, a copy of the log is stored as `<yourmapname>.txt` inside the folder where your `.vmf` file is saved. Instead of reading through the entire log, search for the **LEAK** string.

You will see ****leaked**** wherever the compile tools detected a leak, as shown in the following screenshot:

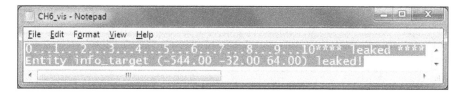

It can be a pain to track down the origin of a leak, but the compile tools make it a bit easier by creating a **pointfile** whenever it detects a leak. The **pointfile** traces the lighting path starting at a source entity and ending in the void. If your map has a leak, you can load the **pointfile** by navigating to **Map | Load Pointfile**. Look at the compile log to see where the source entity is, and trace the red **pointfile** entity line to the source of the leak. In this example, the **info_target** entity shows us the leak is coming from an unsealed skybox.

The compile log is useful for more than just leak checking; it will list other errors as well with hints on how to resolve them. Also listed in the compile log is the time it takes for each step to complete (BSP, VIS, and RAD), and based on what you would like to watch, the compile window will show you which step of the process it's on. The log also shows how full the map is. Since this is a computer game, and not real life, you have to work within limits. Check out the compile log to see how much space you have left for light data, entities, brush faces, and more.

Cubemaps

Cubemaps allow all the normal and bump-mapped materials in your maps to reflect light properly. They are also necessary for proper water rendering and making sure your weapons reflect the proper parts of the world. To see the effects of a **cubemap** in the best possible way, let's check out some before and after pictures in the following image:

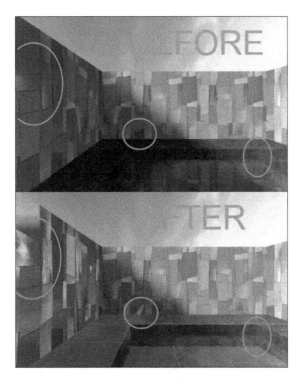

In the before shot, the water looks pretty, and it is reflecting the wall. However, overall the wall looks flat and dark. Once a cubemap is placed into a map, you can immediately tell the difference. In the circle on the left, you can see the reflection of the sky in the wall. In the center circle, there is a reflection of a green light located behind the player. In the right circle, you can see the reflected upper wall and the refracted bottom wall beneath the water's surface.

Cubemaps are placed into the world with the **env_cubemap** entity. A good rule of thumb is to place one cube map in each room, one cubemap in each hallway, and to keep the cubemaps about 64 units off the ground (that is, the eye level). Cubemaps also need to be at least 16 units away from any brushes and can also be put in differing areas of color or brightness.

Larger rooms or open areas should have multiple cubemaps. Once the cubemaps are placed in the map, you need to run the `buildcubemaps` console command while in-game to calculate all the reflections. After sending the command, you will see your screen flash with the views of each cubemap. Once this is complete, the map will restart and you will see all your changes.

Adding color correction

Games using the **Source 2009** engine and newer have **color correction** capabilities. This allows you to adjust color, contrast, and shadow depth in real time in the game. This means no compiling in between tweaks! If you think your lighting looks pretty good, but there's something missing, then place a **color_correction** entity into your map so you can fine tune it in the game.

Like other triggerable entities, the color correction entity doesn't need a name unless you want to trigger it on or off. For now, set both of the falloff parameters to **-1** so that the color correction spans the map, compiles your map, and loads it. Once you have your map loaded, walk into the radius of your **color correction** entity, and enter **colorcorrectionui** in the console to bring up the **Color Correction tools**.

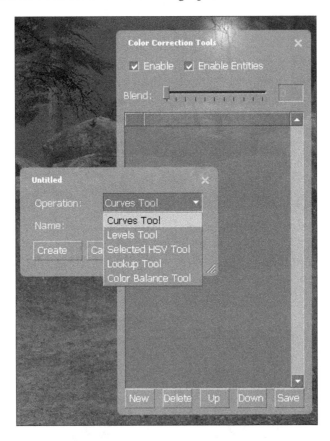

Have a look at the preceding image. Clicking on **New** will give you a new color-balancing effect. **Curves** lets you set the RGB luminosity curves. **Balance** lets you balance the colors in the mids, highs, and lows. There are many other tools available, but the best thing to do is play with them all to get a certain effect. The simplest tool to use is the **balance** tool because you can see the effect very easily.

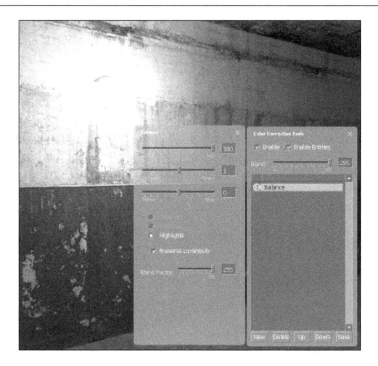

Move the sliders around to view the corrected scene in real time. When you're happy with the result, save the RAW file into your base folder and go back to Hammer. Open the **color_correction** properties and type the name of the raw file you just created in the **Lookup Table Filename** property. When you run the game, the colors will be shifted to get you the perfect lighting you wanted!

Feel free to adjust the falloff radii to the desired distances to fade in and out of the color correction effect.

Summary

Lighting is pretty simple once you break down the individual entities into their specific uses. Point lights are great for adding little details or filling up the whole room with light. Spot lights can be used for a variety of things such as fluorescent lights or prop flood lights. Props and sprites can enhance your lighting and help to provide some added realism. You also now know the difference between LDR and HDR lighting and how to fix leaks or problems, if any, that arise during development. Cubemaps are necessary for having proper reflections, and color correction helps to add that last bit of detail while tweaking the final stages of your maps. One of the best ways you improve the lighting in your maps is to tweak it until you get pretty close, and then add some color correction in the final stages.

Let's move on to the input/output system. Things are just starting to get interesting.

7
Triggers and the Input/Output System

The **Input/Output** system is the heart and soul of any scripting event created with Hammer. An entity is activated or triggered with an **input**. An input tells the target entity what to do; if the target entity is a light, an input could turn the light on or off. Entities have **outputs** as well. If a button is pressed, one of its outputs can tell the light to turn on or off. Inputs trigger outputs. Each entity also has a subroutine-like function that can trigger a sequence of events when told to do so.

In this chapter, we will cover:

- Creating your first triggers
    - Using trigger once
    - Using Trigger multiple
- Using logic triggers
- Using filters
- Using subroutines

Mastering the Input/Output system takes no time at all. Let's jump in.

Creating your first trigger

A trigger, vaguely, is any external input that causes an event or a series of events to start. Walking into a pre-defined area can cause a door to open. Using a button can turn on a light. Shooting at an enemy soldier can cause more soldiers to shoot back at you. All these situations are examples of triggers, and these triggers are handled with Source's Input/Output system. One of the simplest things we can do with the Input/Output (I/O) system is open a door with a **trigger_once** entity.

Creating a trigger once entity

A **trigger_once** entity is a brush-based entity that will initiate a sequence of events (fire outputs), when it collides with the player. So our trigger's input will be the player colliding with the brush, and our trigger's output will be opening a door.

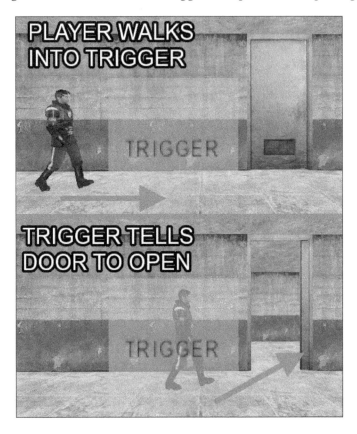

Create two rooms with a door-textured brush separating them. Turn the door-textured brush into **func_door** entity and then let's take a quick look at the **func_door** properties.

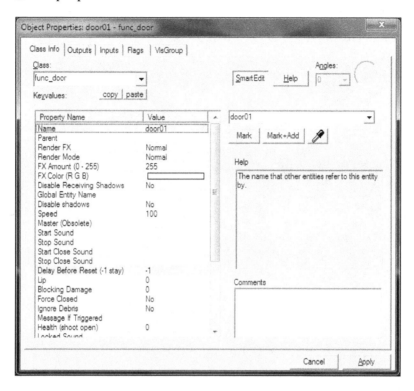

Giving an entity a **Name** allows the I/O system to reference it and control it, so the first thing we should do is call this door **door01**. The **func_door** entity is a sliding door, and it will move in a direction that is set by the **Angles** Property.

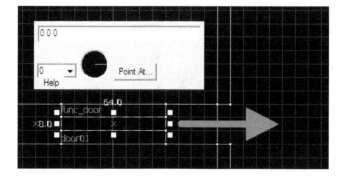

In this example, the **Angles** are set properly by default. **Door01** will move into the wall allowing you to walk through the doorway, but we got lucky. The black circle directly corresponds to the direction of movement in top (x/y) window. Drag your cursor around the black circle to set the door opening angle you desire.

Let's move on to creating the trigger brush.

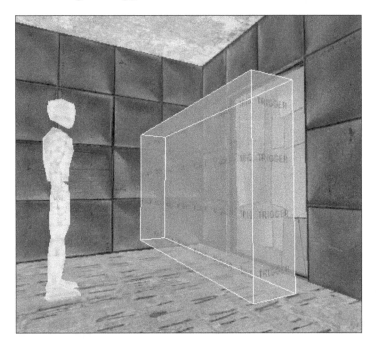

Create a brush in front of the door that the player has to walk through in order to get to the door. Texture the brush with the **tools/trigger** texture and press the **toEntity** button to make it to a **trigger_once**. You have just created a **trigger brush**!

A trigger brush is simply a brush textured with the **tools/toolstrigger** texture that is tied to a trigger entity. An object, player, NPC, or physics object that collides with the trigger will activate one of the trigger's outputs.

The **tools/toolstrigger** texture, as well as any other **tools/*** texture will not render in-game, so don't worry about seeing it once the map is compiled.

Open the properties of this **trigger_once** entity so we can tell it to open our **func_door** entity. We don't need to give this **trigger_once** entity a name, so we can move straight into the **Outputs** tab.

Adding outputs to a trigger once

When triggred, we want our **trigger_once** entity to tell **door01** to open. Sounds simple enough right? It is almost that simple! Here's what we need to do:

1. Choose how this output is activated.
2. Choose the affected entity.
3. Choose the affected entity's action.
4. Specify a time to wait before performing the action.

Our first step is to add an output to the trigger with the **Add** button. The **My Output Named** parameter specifies what type of action will trigger the event. Since this is just a simple trigger, choose **OnTrigger** to fire the output when the trigger is activated.

 The **My Output Named** list is entity specific so it will not be consistent across entities.

The second step is choosing which entity we want to affect with this trigger. You can manually type the entity name, select it from the drop-down list, or use the eye-dropper tool to select the entity the 3D viewport. Whichever way you choose to select the door, set **door01** as the **Target Entity**.

Once we have a **target entity**, our third step is to choose an **input**, or action, we want the entity to perform. Just like outputs, inputs are entity specific too, and in the case of our **func_door** entity, we want it to **Open**.

All triggers can have a **Time Delay** before the action is initiated. We want to open this door immediately, so keep the **After delay in seconds of** field at **0**.

Click on **Apply** to save the changes and take a look at your output you have just created:

```
On Trigger, Door01, Open, 0.00s delay
```

That's almost plain English! As you can see, the output system is pretty easy to use and understand. Compile and run the map to see the door open as you walk up to it. If your **func_door** entity is the same width as your door frame, your will get a render glitch when the door face is on the same plane as the door frame plane. Change the **Lip** parameter in the **func_door** properties to fix this.

Creating a trigger multiple

You'll notice that when triggered, the door will open. The door will automatically close as well. If you didn't' make it through the doorway before the door closed, you're out of luck because you can only open the door once. If we want to be able to open the door multiple times, we need a **trigger_multiple**. If we want the door to stay open indefinitely after triggering, set the Delay before close property to -1.

Trigger_multiple acts almost the same as **trigger_once**, but it can be activated multiple times. Turn the **trigger_once** into a **trigger_multiple** so we can how this all works.

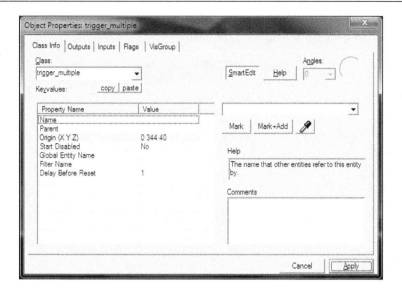

Again, the main difference between a **trigger_once** and a **trigger_multiple** is the fact that a **trigger_multiple** can be activated more than once. **Trigger_multiples** have a field called **Delay Before Reset** that controls how often the trigger can be activated. Compile and run your map with the **trigger_multiple** and you will see that you can open the door in intervals specified by the **Delay Before Reset** property.

Input/Output links

If you open any entity that has an output assigned to it, you will see that there is now an icon containing a dot with an arrow coming out of it located in the bottom left corner of the properties window.

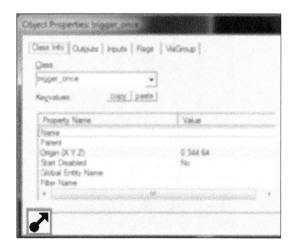

This icon tells us that this entity has an output assigned to it. You can double-click on any specific output to jump to the target entity's **Inputs** tab.

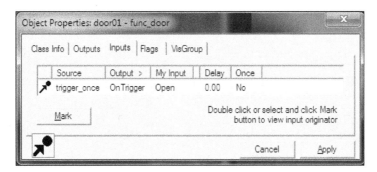

In bottom-left corner of the **func_door**'s properties, you can see that there is a picture of an arrow pointing to a dot. This signifies that this entity has an input. Again, double-clicking on the input will jump to the triggering entities' properties. Every entity's output creates an input somewhere else. And you can easily see if an entity has an input or output based on these icons.

Cascading triggers

Outputs have time delays built into them. While it is possible to have one entity control a whole series of events with set time delays, it is often cumbersome to perfectly time everything. Let's say we want a light to turn on in the second room two seconds after the **func_door** entity is open. We could tell the **trigger_once** entity to have a second output that tells the light to turn on in about 2.5 seconds, (adding half a second for door travel time), or we can simply have the **func_door** entity turn on the light once it is fully open. A **cascade** occurs when an entity receives an input and triggers another entity via an output when its input action is complete.

Create a light in the second room and name it room02_light01. In the **Flags** tab of the light, select **initially dark** so it starts off and we need to tell the light to turn on.

Now open the **Outputs** tab of the **func_door** entity and add a new output. When the door is fully open, turn on the light in the next room after two seconds. Your output should look like the following:

```
OnFullyOpen, room02_light01, TurnOn, 2.00s delay
```

Hit **Apply** to save the changes, then give the map a test compile to check the results.

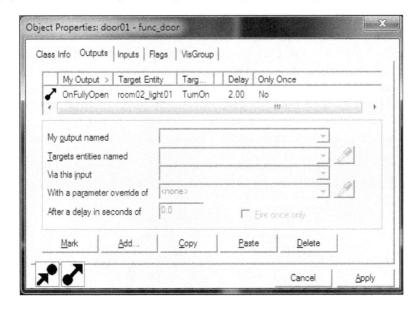

Our **func_door** entity has both the input and output icons in the bottom-left corner which means this entity has both inputs and outputs.

Automatic triggers

If you want something to happen as soon as you start a map, or as soon as you load from a save file, there is an entity for that. The **logic_auto** entity fires an output based on level start conditions.

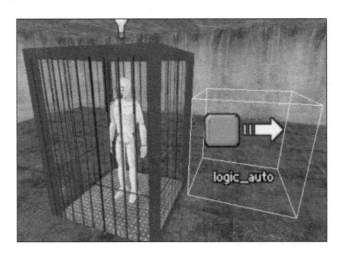

In this case, I have surrounded the player start with a **func_door** entity in the shape of a cage. I have set an output in the **logic_auto** to open the door (lower the cage into the floor) after the map has been loaded for five seconds. The output is as follows:

```
OnMapSpawn, cage01, Open, 5.00s delay
```

My Output >	Targ...	Tar...	Delay	Only Once
OnMapSpawn	cage01	Open	5.00	No

Modifying entity effects

A great feature of the Source engine is the ability to control special entity properties such as **render modes**. We can dynamically change parameters such as the **alpha**, or transparency of entities. We can manipulate two overlapping light model's alpha to trick the player into believing a light model is actually casting light when the point light beneath it turns on. If a model has a skin, it can easily be changed by sending a **skin = number** input, but some entities don't have different skins so we need to play some tricks with the render modes.

Place a **prop_dymanic** entity on the ceiling above the light in the second room and name it room02_light01_mdl_off. Assign the **prop_dynamic** entity the **light_domelight02_off.mdl** model and change its **render mode** to solid.

The entity name might seem long, but following a consistent naming convention will help you will stay organized, and it could make your life much easier when your maps have lots of entities. Assigning the prop a render mode of **solid** will let us change the **alpha** property with triggers. Make a copy of the **prop_dynamic** entity by holding *Shift* and dragging it and rename it to room02_light01_mdl_on.

Assign the copied **prop_dynamic** the **light_domelight02_on.mdl** model and set the **FX amount** to 0. When **FX amount** of a solid-rendered model is 0, it will be invisible when the map is first loaded. When **FX amount** is **255**, the model will be 100 percent opaque. Any value between these two values will render the model as semi-transparent.

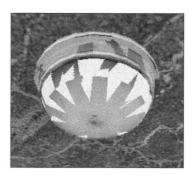

Rendering artifacts occur when multiple objects occupy the same planes. The preceding screenshot was taken within Hammer, but the same effect occurs within the game. We don't have to worry about this artifact occurring in game because our triggers prevent both models from rendering at the same time.

When the light is off, we want the **on** model to have an **alpha** target of **0**, and we want the **off** model to have an **alpha** of **255**.

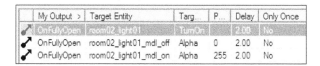

When the light is on, we want the **on** model to have an **alpha** of **255**, and the **off** model to have an **alpha** of **0**.

 We can remove the **off** model from the world by passing the **Kill** input. Because this light is triggered via a **trigger_once** entity, the light will remain on permanently, and there is no reason to keep the **off** model anymore. Since **prop_dynamic** entities require a relatively large amount of resources, killing them can help the game run smoother. Passing the **alpha** parameter will keep the model in the map, and we will retain the ability to change the render states in the future.

Thus, we have not been using the **Parameter Override** field in our outputs because we have not triggered anything that required a parameter setting. When we send the **alpha** command to an entity, we need to specify the amount of **alpha** we want the model to render with. Placing a number between 0 and 255 into the **parameter override** field will control the render amount.

Using different flags

Triggers have **flags** that can be set to specify what entity type can trigger them. Check the box to select which entity type can activate the trigger. Any trigger defaults to allowing only **clients** (players) to activate them, but this can easily be changed to allow or forbid multiple activator types.

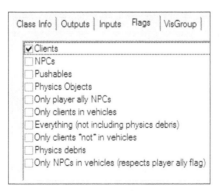

As an example, if you want a window to break if you throw a rock at it, put a **trigger_once** entity in front of a **func_breakable** entity (named window01) and set the flags of the **trigger_once** entity to **Physics Objects** only.

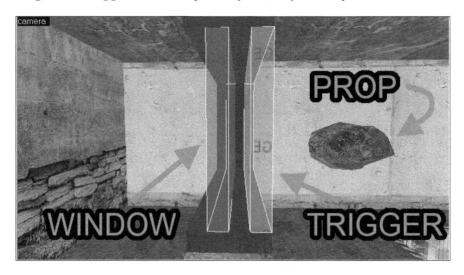

The output obtained for the **trigger_once** entity would be as follows:

```
OnTrigger, window01, Break, 0.00s delay
```

The window will break if any physics object, such as a rock, touches the trigger, but it will not break if the player touches the trigger.

Using filters

We can provide even more control over which objects or NPCs trigger which event using **filters**. Filters help to tell a trigger which entities can or cannot affect them. The **filter_activator_class** entity, for instance, will check the activator's class name against its setting and will only let the trigger fire if the class names match.

[An activator is anything that activates a trigger and the class is the type of entity, not the name.]

The following flowchart will explain the logic of the sequence:

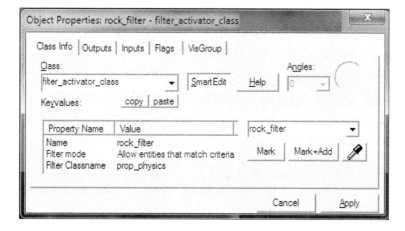

Using the previous example of throwing a rock at a window, create a brush with a window texture and tie it to a **func_breakable** entity. Name it window01 and in the **Flags** tab, check the **only break on trigger** box to ensure that only a triggered input can make it break. Create a trigger brush in front of the window that the rock must pass through. Check only the **Physics Objects** box in the **Flags** tab and then create the following output:

```
OnTrigger, window01, Break, 0.00s delay
```

Create the **filter_activator_class** point entity and name it rock_filter. In the **Filter Classname** property, type prop_physics to allow only **prop_physics** entities to break the window.

In the **trigger_once** properties, set the **filter** parameter to `rock_filter` to allow the trigger to look for the **prop_physics** trigger.

Now, we need to create the two different types of physics objects so that we can see the filter in action. You already know about **prop_physics** entities, but there is another physics object known as a **func_physbox** entity. A **func_physbox** or a **physbox** entity is a brush or group of brushes tied to a **func_physbox** entity that will respond to the physics engine in the game. Create a **prop_physics** entity using the **rock_forest01b.mdl** model, and then create a **sphere** brush and tie it to a **func_physbox** entity.

Our **trigger_once** brush will use this filter to determine which entity name or entity type is allowed to trigger an input. In the **trigger_once** properties, assign **Filter Name** to **rock_filter**.

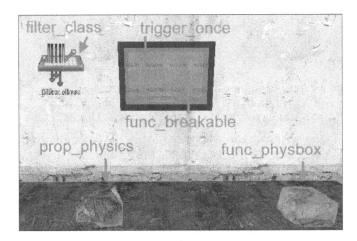

Our entity setup is now complete and we can test it in-game! You can throw the **func_physbox** entity at the window until your finger gets a cramp, but it will never break the window because the filter tells the trigger to ignore the incorrect activator. Toss the **prop_physics** entity at the window; however, the window will break immediately, allowing the rock to pass through to the other side.

The filter activator name

Activator_name filters act just like the **Activator_class** filters except that the **filter_activator_name** filter looks for a specific entity *name* instead of a generic entity *class*. Using the **filter_activator_name** entity, you can set a trigger's flag to `everything` to allow all types of entities to activate the trigger. The **filter_activator_name** entity will only allow entities of a certain name to actually have any effect on the trigger. Look at the example map to see this in action.

The filter multi entity

Filter_multi entities have the ability to perform logic operations with existing filters. A **filter_multi** entity will compare up to five existing filters and then decide what the outcome should be. There are four different logic operations that can be performed:

- **And (Logic type: And, Negate outcome: No)**: An And operation will compare two or more inputs and only trigger an output if all inputs are satisfied.

- **Nand (Logic type: And, Negate outcome: Yes)**: A Nand operation will negate the And operation; the output will always trigger unless all the inputs are satisfied.

- **Or (Logic type: Or – Negate outcome: No)**: An Or operation will trigger an output if any one of the inputs are satisfied.

- **Nor (Logic type: Or – Negate outcome: Yes)**: A Nor operation will only trigger an output if all inputs are not satisfied.

Filter_multi entities are implemented just like the other filter entities such that you enter the filter name into a trigger's **filter** property.

Creating subroutines

Every entity, regardless if it possesses specific outputs, can be used to fire a sequence of events via the **FireUser** input. The **FireUser** input can be related to a subroutine. **FireUser** inputs are useful for complex entity setups that can be triggered multiple times in a cascading fashion.

In the example map provided, there is a **env_explosion** entity **parented** (attached) to a **prop_physics** garden gnome. There is a **point_teleport** entity that teleports the garden gnome on the pedestal behind the glass. There is a **trigger_multiple** entity behind the button that controls and teleports the gnome to the pedestal and fires a series of explosions to bounce the gnome around the room. Since the **env_explosion** entity is parented to the gnome, wherever the gnome is, the **env_explosion** entity is in the same relative position. The button on the post tells the trigger to use **FireUser1**, and the **trigger_multiple** entity activates all the outputs relative to the **User1** input.

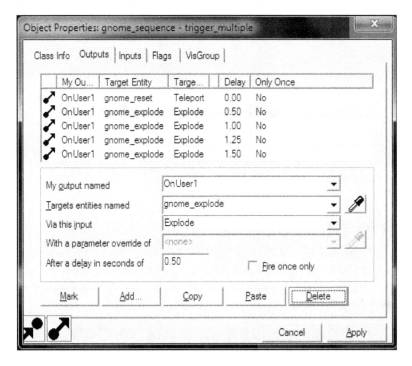

Now, any other entity can tell the **trigger_multiple** entity to trigger **FireUser1** and instead of triggering six separate events, only one event needs to be triggered.

Summary

Hammer's Input/Output system is an incredibly versatile tool that is very simple to use and understand. Each entity class has a multitude of different inputs and outputs that can be activated with simple trigger entities. **Trigger_once** entities fire outputs once while **trigger_multiple** entities trigger some things as many times as you want. Filters are powerful tools that let you control exactly which events are triggered by which entities. Now that you know how to harness the power of the input/output system, let's have some fun with cameras and track trains!

8
Trains and Camera Systems

The Half-Life series of games have a strange affinity for trains. There was an entire chapter devoted to them in Half-Life. Half-Life 2 starts you out on one train, almost kills you on another, and the player is on the same train in between Half-Life 2 episodes 1 and 2. The Source SDK contains a powerful set of tools devoted to make objects move. If you want full control over that movement, you'll want to use a train. Half-Life focuses on first-person story development, but it still has moments where the view is taken over by a secondary camera. Combining trains and cameras can make for powerful storytelling cutscenes.

In this chapter, we will learn:

- Creating and controlling track trains
- Creating a security system using cameras
- Combining trains and cameras to make cut scenes

There are some exciting topics to be covered in this chapter, so let's jump in!

Track trains

Track trains are brush-based entities that move forward and backward along a **path**. The path that track trains follow is made up of linked point-based **path_track** entities. Track trains come in two main varieties: **player-controlled** and **automatic**. Player controlled track trains, when used, override the player's forward and backward movement keys to control the train movement. These trains can be ridden and have the ability to switch the path they take with external triggers. Automatic track trains are controlled with external triggers and have no *direct* player control. An example of an automatic track train could be a platform with more than one movement direction or, as we'll soon see, an invisible box acting as a camera's target.

Player-controlled track trains

Func_tracktrain entities have the ability to be player controlled. These are brush-based entities that the player must be standing on in order to be controlled. There are three main parts to a player-controlled **func_tracktrain**:

- **Func_tracktrain**: This is the moving object made of world brushes.
- **Func_traincontrols**: This is the trigger brush that controls the forward and backward movement of the train. The player must stand on the train and be inside this brush.
- **Path_track**: This defines the path that the train will follow.

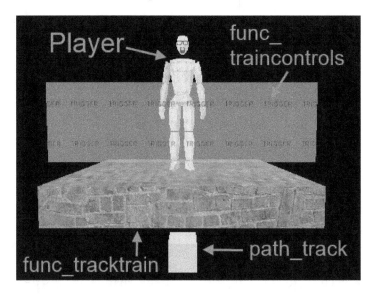

Creating the func_tracktrain entity

Create a brush and tie it to a **func_tracktrain** entity. The train brush can be of any shape or size so long as the player can stand on it. When creating the **func_tracktrain** entity, the front of the train must face east (facing to the right if looked at from the top 2D viewport). Name it `func_tracktrain01` and set the **Is Unblockable by Player** flag to `true` so the train won't stop if it runs into the player. (This flag can cause some buggy behaviour if not checked.) When the train is spawned in the game, the train **origin** will be located at the **start pointpath_track** entity and the front of the train will be facing the second **path_track** entity. Change the **Render Mode** option to `Not Rendered` so the train will be invisible in the game.

Instead of playing with render modes, you can also texture the track train with the **tools/toolsinvisible** texture to achieve the same effect.

Creating the path

Now, let's create a path with two nodes for our train to travel between. Place two **path_track** point entities in the map. Name one `path_tracktrain01_start` and name the other `train01_end`. In the properties of **train01_start**, set the **Next Stop Target** field to `train01_end`. When the train is told to move forward, it will move in a straight line towards the **train01_end** entity.

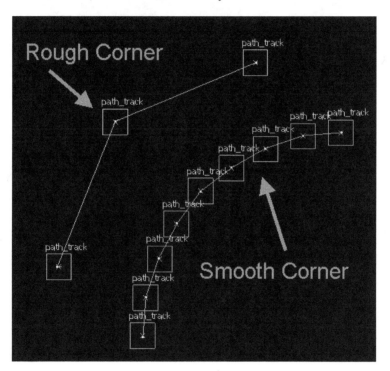

If you copy a **path_track** entity (by holding *Shift* and dragging it) that already has a name, the new **path_track** entity will inherit the original name but have a number appended to it. The original will have the **Next Stop Target** field set as the new **path_track** entity. The technique of holding *Shift* and dragging it to make a copy of **path_tracks** is a quick and easy way to create a path with any number of nodes. Since trains move in a straight line between **path_tracks**, it's easy to use this technique to create smooth corners by following the edge of a cylinder; the more sides on the cylinder, the smoother the corner will be.

When you give a **path_track** entity a **Next Stop Target**, an orange line will be drawn between the two entities to show you the path of travel as shown in the following figure:

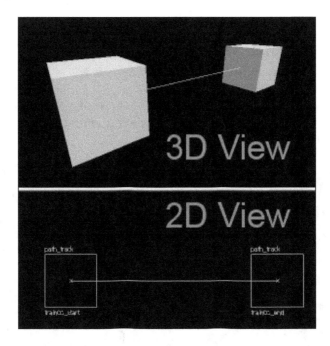

We didn't give **train01_end** a **Next Stop Target** so when the train arrives at this **path_track**, the train will stop moving. If the train is told to move in reverse, it will move toward **train01_start**.

Tying the track train to the path

Open the properties of your **func_tracktrain** entity and set the **First Stop Target** field to **train01_start** so the train's origin will be at **train01_start** when the map spawns.

Normally, the origin of any brush-based entity is located in the centre of the brush (or group of brushes if your entity is made up of multiple brushes). You can change the location of a brush-based entity's origin by moving the white origin circle when the **Toggle helpers** button in the top toolbar is clicked.

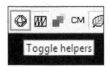

In the 3D viewport, an object's origin is indicated by a purple sphere.

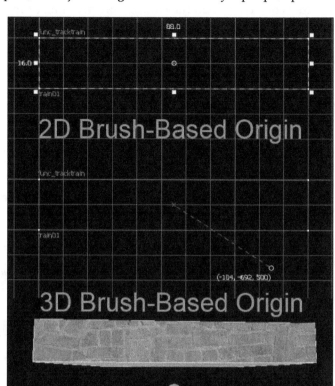

An object's origin controls many things. In the case of a track train, the origin controls the pivot, and the track train will move along its path based on its origin.

The controls

So far we have a train and a path but we do not have any means of controlling the train. We need to place the train controls now. Create a trigger brush above the **func_tracktrain** entity and tie it to the **func_traincontrols** entity. **Parent** it to the **func_tracktrain** entity (so it always moves with it) and set the **train name** property to the train as well (**train01**).

Now you can run the map to test your train. Press the use button while standing on the train to activate the controls. When the controls are activated, press the forward and backward movement keys to control the train. The maximum forward speed is specified by the **Max Speed** property, while the maximum reverse speed will be one quarter of the **Max Speed** value.

Adding detail

Right now, the train is boring and plain. You can create a more visually interesting train with brushes, or you can parent models to the train for added detail. In the example map (ch8_tracktrain), there is a train cart and a combine control panel parented to a **func_tracktrain** entity. The player still stands on the **func_tracktrain** entity (so the train controls will work) but it is not rendered, giving the illusion that the player is actually standing on the model.

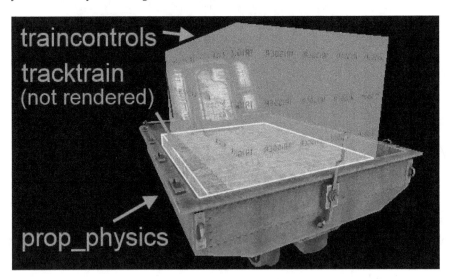

Branch paths

A **branch path** is the secondary **Next Stop Target** that is enabled or disabled with an external trigger (explained later). A branch path will allow the train to go to an alternate **path_track** that leads to another direction. This can be useful to control which direction the train will turn at an intersection.

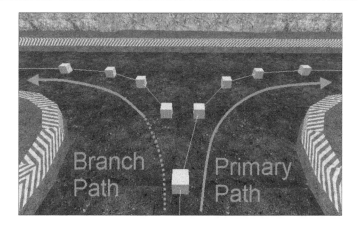

The connections between branch paths are not shown in 2D or 3D views as regular **next_stop_targets** are. If you have a lot of branch paths in your map, this could get quite confusing.

Controlling entities with GameUI

A player does not *need* to be standing on a train to control it. You can give button outputs to tell the train to startforward, startbackward, or stop, or we can mimic the **func_traincontrols** functionality with a *gameui* without a complicated array of buttons. A **gameui** directly reads keyboard and mouse inputs, and fires outputs based on the keys pressed.

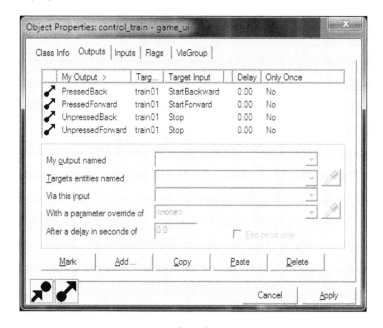

A **func_button** entity can activate a **gameui**, and then the **gameui** compares the forward and backward movement keys. When the forward key is pressed, the train moves forward and when it stops being pressed, the train stops. When the backward key is pressed, the train moves backwards and the train stops when the key is released. Trains aren't the only entity that can be controlled this way; experiment!

Trains are one of the more useful brush entities in the game. They can move in any direction, rotate to face the direction of movement, or simply maintain a fixed orientation. They can be player-controlled or trigger-controlled and the player can even ride on them. The next section describes cameras and we'll see how trains and cameras can be combined to create a cutscene.

Point camera

Point_camera entities project an image onto a **monitor**. These can be useful to simulate a TV broadcast, video call, or security camera system. There are three main parts to a **point_camera** system:

- Camera (**point_camera**)
- Monitor (any brush-based entity)
- Camera link (**info_camera_link**)

The **point_camera** entity is the actual camera. You simply give it a name and aim it at whatever target you want it to look at. The monitor is a special texture that will display the **point_camera**'s image, and the **info_camera_link** entity specifies which camera is displayed onto the monitor texture. Let's walk through creating a simple security system.

Create a two-room map with a light in each room. In one room, place a **point_camera** entity and something for it to look at. Name the **point_camera** entity sec_cam01 and click on the **look at** button to easily set the camera's target. In my example, I have the camera looking at an **npc_antlion**.

In the other room, place an **info_player_start** entity and a television-sized brush. Texture the brush with the **halflife/black** texture and tie it to a **func_detail** entity. In front of the black brush, place another brush with a monitor texture on the front, such as **dev_tvmonitor1a**. *Fit* the monitor texture to the front of the brush, and texture every other side with the **nodraw** texture so the image appears only on the front. Tie this monitor brush to a **func_brush** entity and name it monitor_screen.

 Unlike a **func_detail** entity, a **func_brush** entity allows us to assign a name, which we require in order to link the camera to the monitor.

Your television should look somewhat similar to a modern flat screen television:

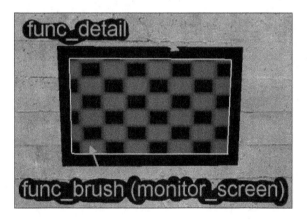

Now to tie everything together, place an **info_camera_link** point entity in the room. Set the **Entity Whose Material Uses_rt_camera** field to the **func_brush** entity name (**monitor_screen** in this case) and set the **camera name** field to the name of the camera, sec_cam01. Name the **info_camera_link** entity camera_link.

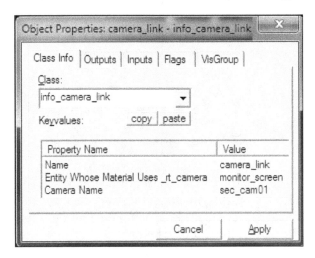

You're all set! Now, when you compile and run the map, you will see an image of an ant lion on the wall.

A one-camera security system isn't that impressive. How about we add another?

Multiple cameras

The **info_camera_link** entity has the ability to change which camera is forwarded to a monitor by passing the **setcamera** input. Create another room with a second **point_camera** entity in it. Name the second camera sec_cam02. Create a **func_button** entity in the control room (the room with the monitor in it). Set the button's **delay before reset** field to -1, and set the **toggle** flag so the button needs to be pressed in, and then manually "pulled" out. Give the **func_button** entity the following outputs:

```
OnIn  > camera_link > SetCamera > sec_cam02 > 0.00s Delay
OnOut > camera_link > SetCamera > sec_cam01 > 0.00s Delay
```

When the button is pushed in, the camera link uses **sec_cam02** as the display camera, and when the button is pulled out, the camera link uses **sec_cam01** as the display camera.

Panning the camera

We can get even fancier with our security camera by parenting a **point_camera** entity to a **func_door_rotating** entity to make our camera pan across a room. Create a small brush behind the **point_camera sec_cam02** entity and tie it to a **func_door_rotating** entity. Name the **func_door_rotating** entity sec_cam02_pan and assign it the following outputs:

```
OnFullyOpen   > sec_cam02_pan > Close > 2.00s Delay
OnFullyClosed > sec_cam02_pan > Open  > 2.00s Delay
```

So when the door is fully open, it will wait for two seconds and then close. Likewise, when the door is fully closed, two seconds will pass and it will open again. Because the **point_camera** entity is parented to the **func_door_rotating** entity, the camera will rotate with it, and look across the room.

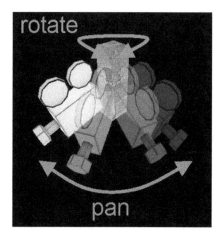

By controlling the **speed** (in degrees per second) and **distance** (in degrees) parameters of the **func_door_rotating** entity, you can fine-tune the coverage characteristics of your security camera.

The outputs we just noted will fire continuously for as long as the map is loaded. However, when the map spawns, the door is in a dormant, closed state and will not fire the **OnFullyClosed** output. We need to manually set things in motion, so place a **logic_auto** entity next to the **func_door_rotating** entity and give it the following output:

```
OnMapSpawn > sec_cam02_pan > Open > 0.00s Delay
```

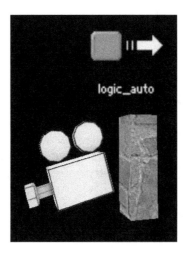

Now that the door is being initialized, it can rely on the outputs to pan indefinitely.

Using these techniques, you can even parent a **point_camera** entity to an NPC for a simulated first person view of whatever that NPC sees. The possibilities are nearly endless.

Point_viewcontrol

Point_camera entities display a camera view on a screen like a television. You, the player, can still walk around and interact with the world while a **point_camera** entity is active. **Point_viewcontrol** entities, by contrast, take over the player's view. The player can still walk around with a **point_viewcontrol** entity active, but there is always the option (**flag**) to freeze the player so they can't walk or look around. These cameras can be told to always look at a specific entity or even the player. **Point_viewcontrols** entities can even move along a path like a train. **Point_viewcontrol** entities are perfect for cutscenes, so let's make one!

The example map `ch8_viewcontrol` has a prebuilt and prescripted entity setup for your reference in this section. In the example map, the level fades in as the camera moves towards a house. When the camera nears the door, it opens to reveal a dead zombie. After scoping out the room, the camera stops at our players' view and we attain control.

The camera

After we create our environment, the first order of business is to place a **point_viewcontrol** and set it up to follow a target. After that's done, we can work on tweaking camera movement and creating our other triggers.

We're first going to create a track train, so make an 8 x 8 x 8 **func_tracktrain** and name it `camera_target`. The camera is going to be pointing at this train, but we don't want it to be visible, so set its **Render Mode** to **don't render**. The next thing we need to do is create a path for our camera to look at; basically a sequence of points of interest where our train will travel to.

Create a **path_track** entity and name it `camera_target_path01`. Copy the **path_track** entity twice (by holding *Shift* and dragging it) to create **camera_target_path02** and **camera_target_path03**. Set the **func_tracktrain's first_stop_target** to `camera_target_path01`.

Now that our camera target and path are set up, let's move on to the camera itself. Place a **point_viewcontrol** entity in the map and name it `camera01`. In the **entity to look at** field, type in `camera_target` so our camera will always look at the **func_tracktrain** entity we have just created.

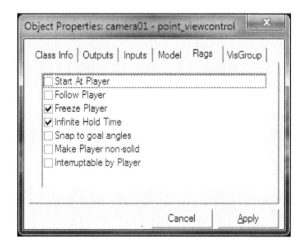

In the **point_viewcontrol** properties, set the flags **Freeze Player** and **Infinite Hold Time** to make sure the player cannot move when the camera is activated and that the camera will stay on until triggered off. Keep all other flags off. Compile the map, run it, and then open the console.

Since we haven't set up any triggers yet, nothing is going to happen, but we can use a console command to control entities as a test. The **ent_fire** command can fire any input of any entity. It can also change render modes, kill entities, and much more. It's a powerful tool that you should spend some time playing with. In this example, we will see how our train functions without the need to interact with triggers.

Type the following commands into the console:

```
Ent_fire camera01 enable
Ent_fire camera_target startforward
```

The first command activates the camera and the second command makes the train move forward. Once the camera is activated, you have no control over your movement or view. This is why we're using the **ent_fire** command to test our entity setup. When the second command is sent, the view will change because an active **point_viewcontrol** entity is pointed to a moving **func_tracktrain** entity.

You'll notice that after you type ent_fire, a list of entities in the map appears in the drop-down list. After you select an entity, all commands related to that entity appear in the drop-down list. If you place a named entity in a map, you can fire different outputs from the console to see what will happen. It's a great learning and troubleshooting tool.

Now that we have the camera activated properly and we are looking at the track train, let's create a path for our camera to travel along.

The camera path

Unlike **func_tracktrains**, **point_viewcontrols** do not follow **path_track** entities; they follow **path_corners**. Thankfully, the **path_corners** function is the same as **path_tracks**, so you already know how to create and link them together.

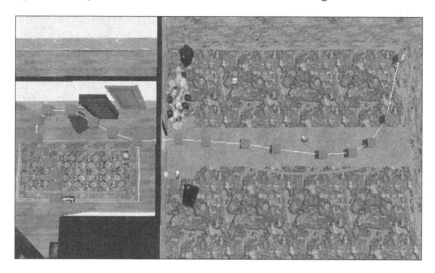

Create a series of **path_corners** entities that will snake around your map and end at an **info_player_start** entity. Place the last **path_corner** entity inside the middle of an **info_player_start** entity, 64 units off the ground. Our goal is to blend the camera movement into the player view as though the camera is moving through the back of the player's head. We want no noticeable difference between the camera view and the player view once the sequence is complete.

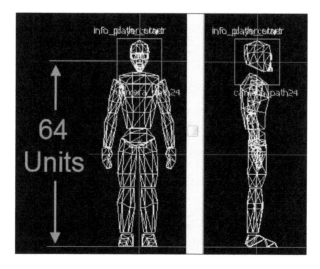

Open the properties of the last **path_corner** entity. Create the following output:

```
OnPass > camera01 > disable > 0.50s Delay
```

Each **path_corner** (and **path_track**) entity will fire the **OnPass** output when an object reaches it. In this case, we want to disable the camera for half a second after it reaches the last **path_corner** entity. With some tweaking, there should be no notable difference in view when the **point_camera** entity turns off.

The speed at which the **point_viewcontrol** entity travels is specified by the **initial speed** parameter in the properties. You can control the speed of the **point_ viewcontrol** entity by putting a non-zero value into the **new train speed** parameter in any **path_corner**. The camera will start moving as soon as it's activated; 50 (units per second) is a good starting value.

Tying it all together

So now we have a camera that moves along a path while looking at a target that is also moving along a path. Syncing the two train timings can prove difficult, so to save time and possible frustration, we're going to cheat. We're not really cheating, but since there are multiple ways of accomplishing the same task, the easiest way is usually the best.

Instead of playing with **track_train** speeds, we're going to make the track train jump, or teleport, from focus point to focus point. We'll do this by firing outputs at certain points in the camera's path. Check the **teleport to this path_track** flag for each node in the **camera_target's** path in order to make that teleport happen. Add the following output to each **path_track** so the track train doesn't keep teleporting away:

```
OnPass > camera_target > Stop > 0.00s delay
```

When the **camera target** entity reaches this point, it will stop moving.

Whenever you want the **viewcontrol** entity to focus on something else, fire an output from one of the path_corners that will start the **camera_target tracktrain** entity.

Select a **path_corner** entity on the camera's path, and add the following output:

```
OnPass > camera_target > StartForward > 0.00s delay
```

Because each **path_track** tells the **camera_target** entity to teleport, you will instantly change the camera's target to the next **path_track** entity.The camera will pan smoothly between **path_tracks**. Compile the map to check out the results!

Summary

The examples in this chapter were just the tip of the iceberg. There's so much you can do with **func_tracktrain** and **point_camera** entities. **Func_tracktrains** can be ridden, hidden, and targeted by other entities. **Point_cameras** and **point_viewcontrols** entities can add another dimension of depth and immersion to your worlds. Making blocks and models move is fun, but the real magic starts to happen when you add NPCs into the mix. NPC movement is next; buckle up!.

9

NPC Movement Basics

Non-playable characters or **NPCs** play vital roles in any video game. Whether they are enemies, allies, bullet fodder, or plot devices, the world would be boring without them. The Half-Life series focuses on story-driven gameplay with the help of NPC interaction. This chapter will provide you with a solid foundation for controlling NPC movement.

In this chapter, we will cover the following topics:

- Familiarizing yourself with the **Model Viewer**
- Making NPCs follow paths
- Controlling NPC animations
- Keeping NPCs busy with minimal scripting

This chapter will take you through some of the different types of NPC movement. For a more detailed look, refer to the example map: ch9_example.vmf. The possibilities are endless, but let's see what we can do!

Using the Model Viewer

One of the many useful tools at your disposal is the Model Viewer. It, like other tools, is located in the bin folder. Because Valve packages all their game files into ZIP-like files called **Valve Pack Files** (**VPK**), we need to unpack the models before we can view them.

Unpacking models

There is a program called **GCFScape** available at `http://nemesis.thewavelength.net/index.php?p=26` that can browse the packed game files and extract them to proper folders. Run GCFScape and open the `hl2_misc_dir.vpk` file in the `hl2` folder located at `common/Half-Life 2`.

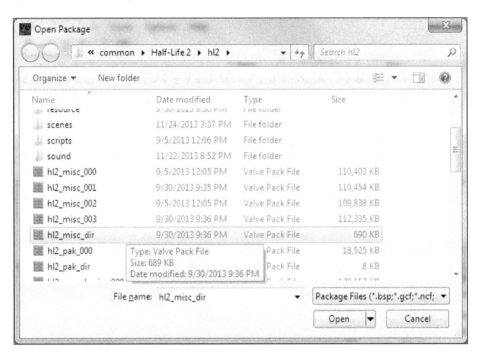

Inside the VPK file, you will see a list of folders that mimic the Steam folder's structure. We want to access the models so we can check out their animations. For this, browse to the `models` folder, and extract the `models` folder to your `common/Half-Life2/hl2/models` folder by right-clicking on it and selecting **Extract**.

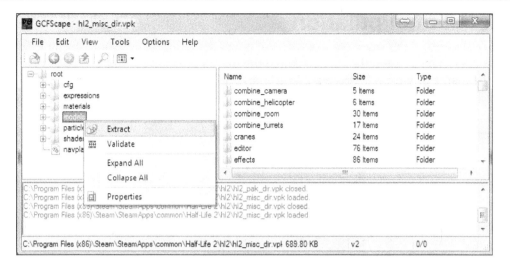

Extract the models folder into the common/Half-Life 2/ep2 folder. A dialog box will appear showing the status of the extraction. Once the extraction is complete, you can close GCFScape.

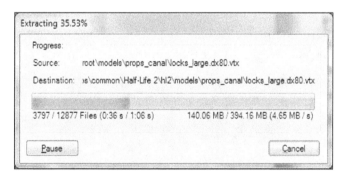

Loading a model

Double-click on the HLMV.bat file in the common\Half-Life 2\bin folder to launch the Half-Life Model Viewer. Go to **File | Load Model** to browse for a model. Browse to the common\Half-Life 2\hl2\models\humans\group01 folder and select male01.mdl.

Model manipulation

When the model is loaded, you can rotate, pan, zoom, and adjust the lighting to get whatever view you would like. To rotate the model along the z and y axis, left-click on the inside of the circle (not visible at first) and move the mouse around. (The dashed circle will turn green when your mouse is clicked inside the circle.)

To rotate the model along the x axis, left-click on the outside of the circle (the dashed outline will now be yellow, signifying that your mouse is outside the circle).

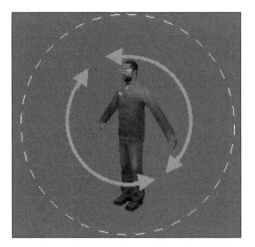

To pan the model around, hold the *Shift* key while left-clicking anywhere on the screen.

Right-click and move the mouse up to zoom in and down to zoom out.

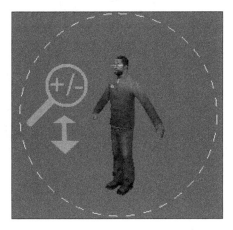

Pressing the *Ctrl* key while left-clicking will move the light source around.

Once you're comfortable with manipulating the view, click on the **Sequence** tab to view a set of animations for that model.

Viewing animations

One of the great things about the Model Viewer is its ability to play models' animations. The **Sequence** tab is where you control the animations you'll see.

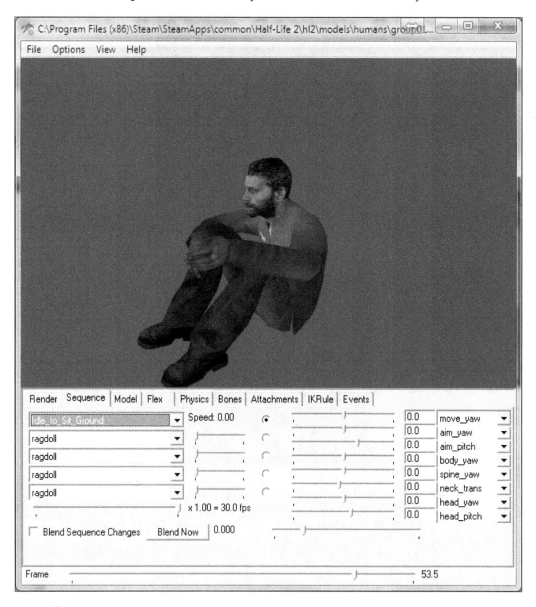

Select an animation from the top drop-down menu to watch the model act it out. There is a slider to the right of each animation selection; manipulating these will blend each selected animation. The slider beneath the drop-down menus controls the speed of the animations.

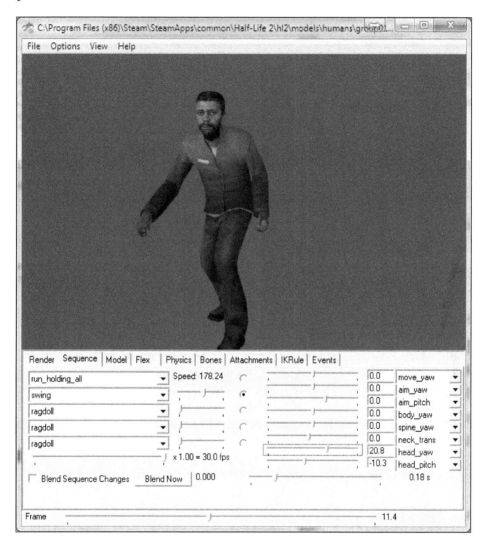

The sliders to the right control other parts of the body not associated with the animations. You can, for example, make the NPC look in a certain direction or change the direction of his torso.

That's all we need to know about the Model Viewer right now. Let's get these NPCs moving, shall we?

Making NPCs walk

NPC movement and reactions are governed by a set of rules known as **Artificial Intelligence** or **AI**. A NPC will walk, run, shoot, or find cover based on a multitude of external stimuli. Each NPC has different AI associated with it.

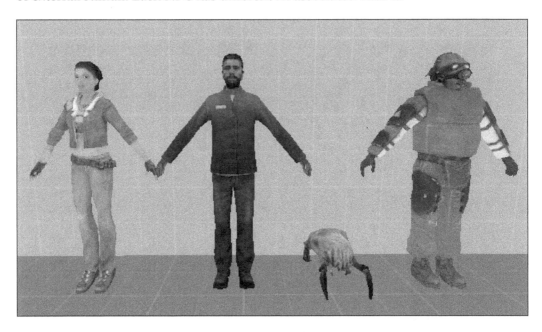

You could place a generic NPC in your map to add some more immersion, yet without scripts, they won't do too much. As an example, combine soldiers and headcrabs will attack if they see you, but citizens will look at you and acknowledge your presence. These are just default behaviors, but thankfully, we don't have to fully rely on plain NPC AI. We can create scripts to get the NPCs to walk, talk more, and interact with the world. Making NPCs walk is quite easy. The **path_corners** entity can be used as navigation points for NPCs. There are two main ways to get an NPC to follow a path: with spawn activity and with an **aiscripted_schedule**.

Simple NPC movement

NPCs can be told to follow a set of **path_corners**, similar to a train, when they spawn. This is useful for populating, say, a busy city street; to add ambience; and simple, simulated random player movement. Controlling NPCs on **path_corners** is quite limited; however, you cannot control the speed of the NPC other than telling them to walk or run.

Place a citizen NPC (**npc_citizen**) in a room along with a **path_corner** entity. Name the **path_corner** path01 and copy it by holding *Shift*, clicking on it, and dragging the copy somewhere else three times to create a four node path.

Assign the fourth **path_corner** a **Next Stop Target** of path01 so it makes a complete loop. The **npc_citizen** entity has a **target path corner** property that will specify where it will move to after being spawned. Once the NPC reaches the first **path_corner**, it will continue to follow the path until it is told to do something else. Because this behavior is automatic, it requires no triggering! As mentioned previously, NPCs follow **path_corners** similar to how a train does. The more **path_corners** you place in a turn, the smoother the movement will be. There are only four **path_corners** in this example, so the **npc_citizen** entity will reach a node, turn 90 degrees, and then continue on towards the next corner.

So we just set up a never-ending loop of mindless NPC movement. What if you want to specifically tell your NPC to move to a point based on a certain set of circumstances? There is no command in an **npc_citizen** input list that will ask it to walk to a specific area. In order to do this, we need to use an entity called **aiscripted_schedule**.

Controlled NPC movement

Aiscripted_schedules can be used for far more than just making NPCs walk. For the time being however, let's experiment with the link between an **aiscripted_schedule** and a set of **path_corners**. Create an **npc_citizen** and a loop of **path_corner** entities. Place a **func_button** on the wall and an **aiscripted_schedule** above the button. This is what we want: when the player uses the button, the NPC will start to walk along the path until it reaches the end. When the NPC reaches the last **path_corner** and finishes walking, the sequence can be restarted.

Since we want full control over the NPC, we should disable some of its AI control before we continue. Open the **npc_citizen** properties and check the following flags: **Ignore Player Push** and **Not Commandable**. Checking **Not Commandable** makes it so the NPC cannot be distracted by using it. **Ignore Player Push** tells the NPC not to move out of the way if you bump into it; the NPC will navigate around you to reach its goal.

The aiscripted_schedule properties

The **aiscripted_schedule** entity assigns goals to NPCs. You can assign enemies as goals, set entity locations as goals, and also set a path as a goal. Since we want our NPC to walk along a path, we set the **Schedule to Run** property to **Walk Goal Path**. This will make the NPC walk towards the **path_corner** specified in the **Goal entity** field and follow the path to the end. The NPC I have created for this script is an **npc_citizen** named meaghan and the path starts at meg_path_01. When activated, this **aiscripted_schedule** will make meaghan walk along the goal path starting with meg_path_01. The **Repeatable** flag is checked so the schedule can be activated multiple times.

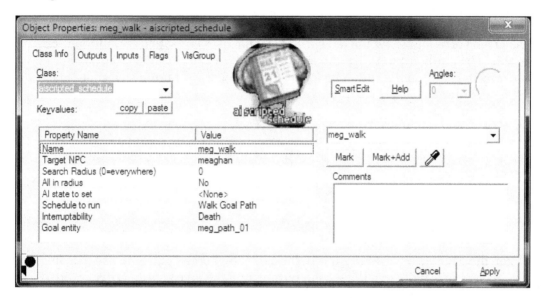

There are a few other parameters we can play with. The **Search Radius** is set to the default value of 0, which will ensure that it searches the entire map for the target NPC. If the NPC is not found, the script will not run. You can set an AI state for the NPC when the script runs. Leaving the **AI state to set** value at its default, None, will not change the current AI; however, you could force a **Combat**, **Alert**, or **Idle** state if you wish. The **Interruptability** controls how this script will stop running. In this case, only the death of meaghan will stop the script, but you can also stop the script if she takes any damage.

Triggering the schedule

In the example map, meaghan is locked in a cell. When the button is clicked, the following actions take place:

```
OnPressed > switch03_active > HideSprite > 0.00s Delay
OnPressed > switch03_not_active > ShowSprite > 0.00s Delay
OnPressed > meg_walk > StartSchedule > 0.00s Delay
OnPressed > button03 > Lock > 0.00s Delay
OnPressed > cell_door > Open > 0.00s Delay
```

There's a lot going on in that button's output, but from top to bottom, here's what's going on and why: there are two **env_sprites** (sprites) next to the button that will tell the player whether the button can be used or not. The first two outputs hide the green sprite and show the red sprite to let the user know that the button is not usable. The third output is the important one; it activates the **aiscripted_schedule** and sets the NPC on the path. The fourth output locks the button so it cannot be used, and the last output opens the cell door so meaghan can leave.

The sequence is complete when the door closes with meaghan in the cell. So this is the perfect place to enable it to be activated again. The very last **path_corner** tells the cell's door to close itself, and when the cell door is closed, the following events happen:

```
OnFullyClosed > button03 > Unlock > 0.00s Delay
OnFullyClosed > switch03_not_active > HideSprite > 0.00s Delay
OnFullyClosed > switch03_active > ShowSprite > 0.00s Delay
```

When the door closes, the button is unlocked, allowing the player to use it again. The red sprite is hidden in the second output, and the green sprite is displayed in the third output letting the player know that the button can be used.

Scripted sequences

Scripted sequences provide more advanced control over NPCs than **path_corners**. They are created with the **scripted_sequence** entity. You can use these for many different actions such as controlling NPC movement and interactions, and for specifying animations. Unlike **aiscripted_schedules**, **scripted_sequences** are location-based entities. NPCs who play a role in the scripted sequence will act out a series of events based on the **scripted_sequence** entity's location. In this example, we're going to make an **npc_citizen** named ben walk across a room and sit in a corner. Place an **npc_citizen** in one corner of a room and a **scripted_sequence** in the opposite corner. Name the NPC ben and name the **scriped_sequence** sequence01.

The **scripted_sequence** controls NPC animations and movement. The NPC will face the same direction the scripted sequence is facing, so if we want ben to look towards the inside of the room, rotate the **scripted_sequence** so the yellow line points inside (alternatively, use the **angles** property to do this). We want to make ben sit down and then stay there, so we need to control two animations: the animation that transitions from standing to sitting and the actual sitting animation. Inside the **scripted_sequence** properties, you will see **Action Animation** and **Post Action Idle Animation** fields. The **Action Animation** plays after the NPC arrives at the **scripted_sequence** location, and the **Post Action Idle Animation** plays when the sequence is complete. We can tick the **loop in post idle** flag to make the **Post Action Idle Animation** play forever. So once ben sits down, he will remain seated forever (playing the sitting animation) until the sequence is cancelled. So our **Action Animation** will be ben transitioning from standing to sitting, and the **Post Action Idle Animation** will be ben sitting on the floor. Let's pick the animations.

Choosing your animation

If you don't know which animations are available or simply don't know the animation name, you can look at each animation in the Model Viewer or the **Model** tab in the **Properties** panel. The quickest and simplest way to choose an animation is to open the **npc_citizen** properties and move to the **Model** tab. In the **Sequence** property, you can select different animations that the NPC will play in the 3D view.

We want ben to sit down, so select the **Sequence** drop-down menu and type in sit to filter the animations so they contain the word sit. In the 3D viewport, the NPC will play the sequence animation so you can exactly see what the NPC will do.

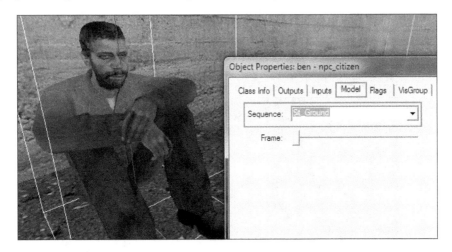

Our **Action Animation** will be idle_to_sit_ground and our **Post-Action Idle Animation** will be sit_ground.

Open the properties of the **scripted_sequence** to apply the following attributes:

- **Name**: ben_sequence01
- **Target NPC**: ben
- **Action Animation**: idle_to_sit_ground
- **Post Action Idle Animation**: sit_ground
- **Move to position**: walk

In the **Flags** tab, check the following:

- **No Interruptions**
- **Override AI**
- **Loop in Post Idle**

Lastly, create a **func_button** to start the sequence with the following output:

```
OnPressed > ben_sequence01 > beginsequence > 0.00s Delay
```

Compile and run the map to watch ben walk across the room, turn to face the center of the room, and then sit in the corner.

Combining sequences

The **scripted_sequence** entity has special outputs that can fire in certain parts of the sequence. Open the **Outputs** tab of a **scripted_sequence** to view all the options available. In this example, we will be linking some **scripted_sequences** together in two ways: **Outputs** and the **Next Script** property. The series of events is as follows: when triggered, Pat (our NPC) will walk to a podium, sit down for 3 seconds, stand up, and walk to a keypad and use it. This sequence will also be repeatable.

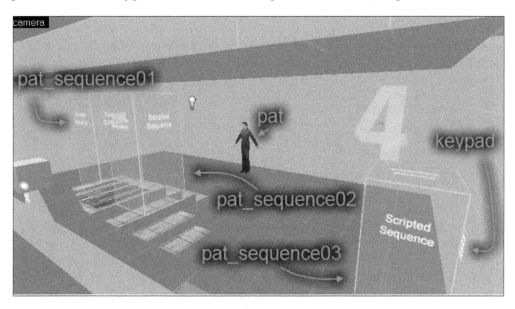

Place two **func_buttons**, an **npc_citizen**, and three **scripted_sequences** in a room. Name the **npc_citizen** Pat (or whatever name you prefer) and name the three scripted sequences Pat_sequence01, Pat_sequence02, and Pat_sequence03. Place Pat_sequence01 at the top of the podium, and place Pat_sequence02 adjacent to it. Place Pat_sequence03 in front of a **func_button** on the wall. Since this is a repeatable sequence, set the **repeatable** flag on each of the **scripted_sequence** entities.

> In my example, I'm setting the NPCs up to spawn with weapons via the **Weapons** property because the sitting and standing animations look odd when the **npc_citizen** does not have anything in their hands.

Name one of the buttons button01 and leave the other without a name.

The `button01` button will set all of our events in motion. Set the **don't move** flag (for aesthetics) and then enter the following output:

```
OnPressed > Pat_sequence01 > BeginSequence > 0.00s delay
OnPressed > button01 > lock > 0.00s delay
```

The first output will activate the first sequence. The other two sequences will be activated by other means. The second output locks the button so we don't have to time the **delay before reset** property. Once the sequences are complete, we will unlock the button so it can be reused.

The **scripted_sequence** `Pat_sequence01` will be similar to `ben` from the previous example. Enter the following properties to have `Pat` walk to the pedestal, sit down, and wait:

- **Name**: `Pat_sequence01`
- **Target NPC**: `Pat`
- **Action Animation**: `idle_to_sit_ground`
- **Post-Action Idle Animation**: `sit_ground`
- **Move to Position**: `walk`

Since we want `Pat` to remain seated once the sequence is complete, check the **loop in post-idle** flag. If this flag is not checked, `Pat` will stand up and return to her default idle stance once the sequence is complete; it won't look pretty either. When the **loop in post idle** flag is checked, the sequence will loop forever until the sequence is canceled. We need to manually cancel the sequence and begin the next sequence after three seconds. Create the following outputs for `Pat_sequence01` to accomplish this:

```
OnEndSequence > Pat_sequence01 > CancelSequence > 3.00s Delay
OnEndSequence > Pat_sequence02 > BeginSequence > 3.00s Delay
```

The second scripted sequence instructs `Pat` to stand up. It has the following properties:

- **Name**: `Pat_sequence02`
- **Target NPC**: `Pat`
- **Action Animation**: `sit_ground_to_idle`
- **Move to Position**: `No - Turn to Face`
- **Next Script**: `Pat_sequence03`

Since we don't want `Pat` to actually move before she stands up, we want to set the **Move to Position** property to `No - Turn to Face`. This will ensure that `Pat` will look in the direction of the **scripted_sequence** angles. In this case, I have set **Angles** to `180` because `Pat` will be facing that direction when she's sitting.

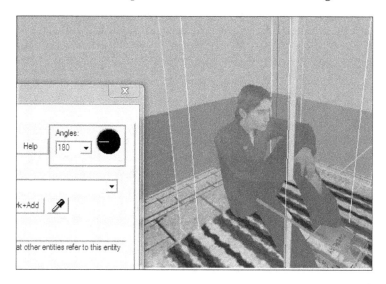

Using the `No - Turn to Face` setting can be useful for activating a series of animations for a single NPC without the need for the **scripted_sequence** to be at the desired NPC position.

The **Next Script** property specifies which **scripted_sequence** to play after this one is complete. The next script will be fired immediately. We have the next script set to `Pat_sequence03`, so as soon as `Pat` stands up, she will begin with the third sequence.

The third sequence tells `Pat` to walk to it and then play the **door open towards left** animation to simulate a button press. The sequence will then fire an output to toggle a **light** in the player's area and reset `button01`.

- **Name**: `Pat_sequence03`
- **Target NPC**: `Pat`
- **Action Animation**: `open_door_towards_left`
- **Move to Position**: `walk`

Add the following output to `Pat_sequence03`:

```
OnEndSequence > light01 > toggle > 0.00s Delay
OnEndSequence > button01 > unlock > 0.00s Delay
```

The first output toggles the **light**. Multiple run-throughs of this sequence of events will turn on and then turn off the light. The second output unlocks the button so it can be used again. Since the firing of this output marks the end of our sequence, we can restart everything.

Actbusy

NPCs have the ability to keep themselves busy without the need for multiple, complex, scripted sequences. The **Ai_goal_actbusy** entity tells an NPC or group of NPCs to keep themselves busy by acting out certain sequences and animations with the help of **info_node_hint** entities. Basically, the **info_node_hint** entity depicts which animations to play, and the **ai_goal_actbusy** entity picks a random node for the NPC to walk to.

In order for the **info_node_hint** to tell an NPC what to do, you need to write a set of instructions that are located in a text file called `actbusy.txt`. This file is located in your `scripts` folder. For example, I'm using *Half-Life 2: Episode Two*, so my `scripts` folder is located at `Steam\steamapps\half life 2`. If you navigate to this folder right now, there might not be anything in it. Again, we'll need to use GCFScape to extract proper files. Extracting files will let us use Valve's `actbusy.txt` file, but we could always create our own. If you create your own `actbusy.txt` file and place it in the `scripts` folder, it will override the packed file and there would be no need to extract the original. For the scope of this tutorial, we will be creating our own `actbusy.txt` file that will instruct our NPCs about actbusy sequences.

Creating the actbusy.txt file

The `actbusy.txt` file contains all the sequences that an **info_node_hint** can reference. It's very simple to create and modify this file once you understand a few basic ideas.

To start, open Notepad (or any other basic text editor) and type the following code:

```
"Actbusy.txt"
{
// SCRIPTS GO HERE
}
```

The very first line defines this text file as the proper `actbusy.txt`. Everything after the first opening curly brace will be an individual script. Comments can be placed in the file to make it easier to read. Any line beginning with a double backslash (//) defines a comment. The closing curly brace completes the document.

Since we've been making our NPCs sit on the floor and are familiar with that set of animations, let's create an actbusy script that will make an NPC sit on the floor for an arbitrary amount of time.

Your first actbusy script

An actbusy sequence is defined in the code like this:

```
"Actbusy.txt"
{
//SEQUENCE ONE
"sequence name"
{
"busy_sequence"    "<busy animation>"
"entry_sequence"   "<entry animation>"
"exit_sequence"    "<exit animation>"
"min_time"         "##.##"
"max_time"         "##.##"
"interrupts"       "<interrupt type>"
}
}
```

The sequence name is almost self-explanatory, but it's the string that references the **info_node_hint**. The busy sequence can be compared with the **Action Animation** of a **scripted_sequence**; however, the busy sequence will be looped for a random period of time between **min_time** and **max_time**. The minimum and maximum time settings are in seconds. The entry sequence is the animation to play before the busy sequence, and the exit animation is played after maximum time has elapsed or the sequence is canceled. You can specify how the sequence is interrupted with the `interrupts` parameter. You can only specify one out of five interrupts for your actbusy sequence:

- **BA_INT_NONE**: This will stop the sequence *only* when the time runs out
- **BA_INT_DANGER**: This stops the sequence if NPC senses danger
- **BA_INT_PLAYER**: This stops the sequence if NPC sees a player *or* senses danger

- **BA_INT_AMBUSH**: Although EP2's `actbusy.txt` says `someone please define this - I have no idea what it does,` it will interrupt the sequence if the NPC sees an enemy

- **BA_INT_COMBAT**: This stops the sequence if NPC sees an enemy or signs of combat such as bullet holes

So if we want to create a script that will make an NPC sit on the floor for 5 to 10 seconds and only lets it get up when the time runs out, the `actbusy.txt` file will look like this:

```
"ActBusy.txt"
{
"sit_on_floor01"
{
"busy_sequence"      "sit_ground"
"entry_sequence"      "idle_to_sit_ground"
"exit_sequence"      "sit_ground_to_idle"
"min_time"         "5.00"
"max_time"         "10.00"
"interrupts"        "BA_INT_NONE"
}
}
```

Save that in your mod's `scripts` folder as `actbusy.txt`.

Making it work

Create a room with an **npc_citizen**, **info_node_hint**, and **ai_goal_actbusy**.

Name the **npc_citizen** `Archie`, give him a weapon (again, purely aesthetic), and set his **not commandable** flag.

Open **ai_goal_actbusy** and modify the following properties:

- **Actors to affect**: `Archie`
- **Start Active**: `yes`
- **Search type**: `Entity name`
- **Search radius**: `2048`

The preceding settings tell only NPCs with the name `Archie` to act busy, and the **search radius** is a decently large `2048` units.

The **info_node_hint** is the last entity we need to modify. Set its properties to the following:

- **Hint**: `world: act busy hint`
- **Hint Activity**: `sit_on_floor01`
- **Node FOV**: `360 degrees`
- **Start Disabled**: `no`

The **Hint type** specifies the action for this node. There are a multitude of choices, each with their own function; however, in order for the actbusy routines to function properly, we need to choose `world: act busy hint`. This will make the hint reference the `actbusy.txt` file we have created. **Hint activity** specifies which actbusy sequence we want to play as specified in the `actbusy.txt` file. Since we only have one possible actbusy sequence, enter `sit_on_floor01`. The **node FOV** can be used to specify which angle an NPC can use it from.

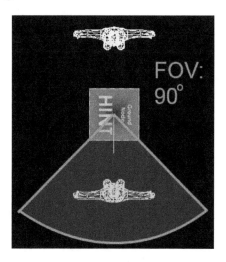

If the **Frame of View (FOV)** is set to 90 degrees, the lower NPC can use the node while the upper NPC cannot. Since we would like Archie to be able to sit on any node from any angle, we want to set this to 360 degrees. The last parameter, **Start Disabled**, is set to no because we want it to be active all the time.

Compile and then run the map to watch Archie sit on the floor for random periods of time.

Actbusy routines can be vastly more complex, but for simple things like this, they don't need to be. If you want to create a slew of random acts for an NPC to carry out in the background, this is the script for you.

Summary

Thus far, you have learned how to control one NPC at a time using **path_corners**, **scripted_sequences**, and actbusy routines. **Path_corner** NPC commands can be controlled with the NPC spawn behavior or with **aiscripted_schedule** entities. **Scripted_sequences** are a fantastic way to bring some more life into NPCs. The next chapter focuses on NPC interaction and squad commands. We'll also be diving into other uses of hint nodes and **aiscripted_schedules**. What are you waiting for?

10
Advanced NPC Scripting

In the previous chapter, we learned how easy it was to give some life to the NPCs in our levels. The Half-Life series of games are classified as First-Person Shooters; what's the fun if we can't get some bullets flying? This chapter will guide you through setting up scripted battles with your NPCs. We could script nearly every footstep of every NPC if we wanted to, but that would take a long time, and the results wouldn't be great unless we spent even more time tweaking every detail. The Source engine has a fantastic AI system that we can manipulate through the use of assaults, squads, and hint nodes. Let's begin.

In this chapter, we will cover the following topics:

- Using hint nodes to guide battles
- Using assaults to assign battle goals
- Using squads
- Setting up lines of defense

Using nodes

The **AI** (**Artificial Intelligence**) is clever, but it frequently needs some coercing to really do what we want it to do. That's where the nodes come into play. Nodes come in many varieties, but we'll be focusing on two nodes in this chapter: info nodes define the basic nav-mesh that the NPCs use to get around and hint nodes give additional meaning to the nav-mesh and help with NPC battles.

Using info nodes

Info nodes, when placed, are short yellow boxes and have **Ground Node** written on them, as shown in the following image:

The **info_node** entity is the most basic piece that makes up the navigation mesh, but they have a significant impact on how the AI works. To really see how necessary these are, let's start by making a simple map where we can see the difference between having them and not having them. Make a 1024 x 1024 room, place some combine soldiers in it, give yourself a gun, and place some boxes for cover. I have included an example map, that is, `ch10_example01` that you can refer to if needs be.

Place a light, compile, then run the map, and fight the combine. Try the map a few times changing tactics every time. You'll notice that the soldiers are pretty static; they don't find cover, they don't chase after you, and they generally seem pretty disorganized.

The battle is easy. You can peek out and shoot them one at a time. The soldiers rarely move, and if they do, it's straight at you, making it easier to pick them off. Go back into the map and, with your entity tool, place some **info_node** entities on the ground at strategic locations. Place them near cover, behind walls, and spread them out in open areas to help guide the soldiers between cover.

The soldiers will use the nodes to navigate around the map. They will travel in a straight line between each node in order to get around. The more **info_node** entities you place, the more options the soldiers have to walk around.

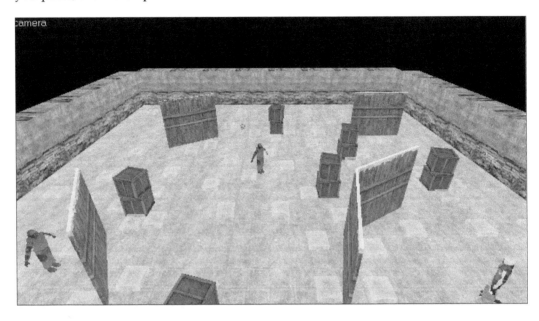

Open the ch10_example02 example map to check out one way to position the nodes. Compile again and then run the map to check out the soldier's new behavior.

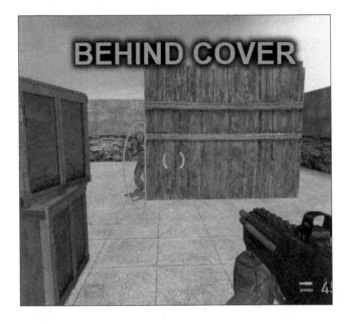

This map just got a bit harder, didn't it? The soldiers are now more aggressive. They don't really give you a chance to breathe, and they're always moving. Not only do they always move around, but also they now take cover behind boxes while reloading and will chase you around a corner if you try to hide.

All we did was place some **info_nodes** entities; how about that? The AI knows to take cover while reloading, and it knows when it can't see you; so, it will try to chase you down. The **info_node** entity gives information about the map to the soldiers, and they allow the AI to really live up to its potential.

Using hint nodes

We can further enhance the effectiveness of the AI by using hint nodes. Hint nodes give some sort of meaning to the area around an NPC and make battles a bit more realistic.

Hint nodes come in two varieties:

- **info_node_hint**: This is a **ground node** that acts like a regular node but with special properties. An NPC can navigate to this node and will act a certain way once there.

- **info_hint**: This is not a **navigation node**, so NPCs won't move to their location, but they can be used to draw attention to certain areas of the map.

The ch10_example03 example map is just like the previous map; only this one has hint nodes stationed behind boxes. These hint nodes will tell the soldiers to crouch behind boxes to take cover.

We've used the same hint nodes for the ActBusy scripts in the previous chapter, but here we're using them a bit differently. Place one down and open the properties, as shown in the following screenshot:

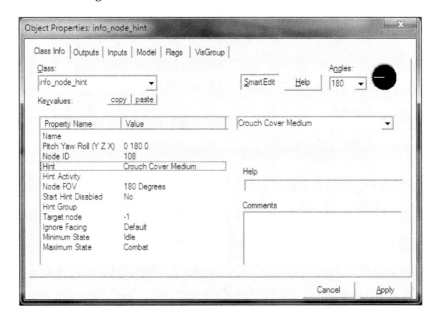

Set the **Hint** parameter to **Crouch Cover Medium**. Any NPC using this node will know that this location is an ideal place to crouch. The **Node FOV** property is a useful property as well. NPCs in the area surrounding this node will only use it if the node can see the target NPC. Take the following image as an example:

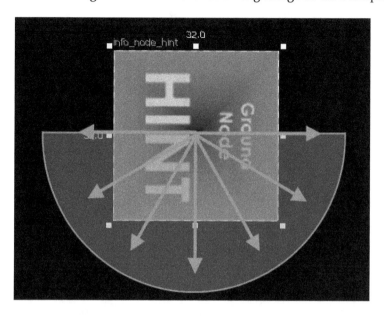

This **info_node_hint** property has an FOV of 180 degrees (90 degrees on either side of the angle it's facing). The NPC will only use this node if it's within the shaded cone.

The **MaximumState** property and **MinimumState** property helps define whether or not an NPC can use a specific node. In this context, a state is defined as **Idle**, **Alert**, or **Combat**. Here, **Idle** is normal behavior; an idle NPC will stand around. An **Alert** NPC has either just exited combat or sensed combat nearby. A **Combat** state is set when there are bullets flying.

For instance, if the **minimum state** is **combat**, and an NPC is not in combat, the NPC will ignore the node. Once we compile and play the game, we can see the effectiveness of the **hint** nodes. The soldiers will actively seek cover if you're shooting at them, making them harder to hit.

That just covers **info nodes** and **hint nodes**. We have proven how useful they are for player versus AI battles. But what about AI versus AI battles? We can do this in AI versus AI battles too.

Scripting assaults

Assaults give the AI a goal. In our last example, the soldiers in the map had one goal—to hunt the player. The nodes we placed in the level helped to guide the AI in both navigation and for seeking defense. We can use the same process to script AI versus AI battles. Load the `ch10_example04` example map to see a house held by citizens and an outside area filled with combine soldiers. You can also create your own scenario if you wish.

The map is littered with info nodes and hint nodes. There are also **hint_nodes** in the windows. These are set to be visually interesting but only for NPCs outside of the house. The FOV is 180 degrees with the hint angle pointing outside the house. We want only the soldiers to focus on the windows so that they will be ready when the citizens appear in them. Run the map and see what happens.

Have a look at the preceding image. You'll notice that the soldiers aren't storming the house, and the citizens aren't going outdoors to meet them. The combine standing outside will move to the closest cover and try to survive while trying to defeat the citizens. The citizens are nice and protected inside the house, so they have no reason to go anywhere. The NPCs can see each other but they have no goals other than killing their visible enemies. The goal we want is for the combine to gain entry to the house. Let's set up what's known as an **assault**.

Setting up an assault

An assault needs at least four entities that are mentioned as follows:

- NPC
- **ai_goal_assault**
- **assault_rallypoint**
- **assault_assaultpoint**

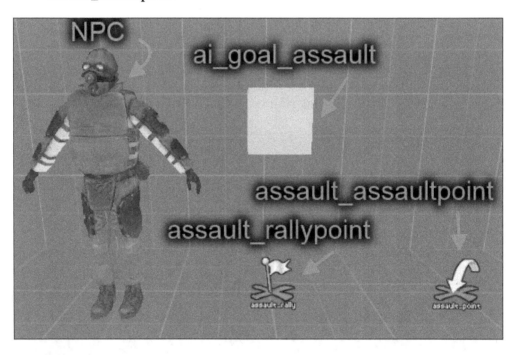

The **assault_assaultpoint** entity is the end destination; it's the point where the assault NPCs will try to reach. The **assault_rallypoint** entity is the area where an NPC will gather before beginning the assault. Once a rally point and an assault point are defined, the rally point entity will draw a purple line towards the assault point it's attached to. The **ai_goal_assault** entity is the master controller; this entity starts and stops the assault. It also gives you control over how aggressive the NPCs are in pursuing their goals. Let's set up our assault so that the NPC soldiers storm the house.

Placing the assault point

The first thing you want to do is place your **assault_assaultpoint** entity. Since we want the soldiers to gain entry to the house, place the **assault_assaultpoint** entity on the floor in the middle of the house, as shown in the following image:

Give it a name such as assault_here and change the **allow diversion** property to **yes**. This setting will still have the soldiers storm the house, but they will do so in a safe manner. They will seek cover and advance only when they can't see an enemy. If the **allow diversion** property is set to **no**, all the 12 soldiers will storm into the house at once. It's funny to watch, and useful in certain scenarios, but it's not exactly what we want to do here.

Placing rally points

An assault can have any number of rally points because each NPC involved in the assault needs its own specific rally point. Place one rally point for each NPC you would like to have. In the ch10_example05 example map, there are 12 soldiers mounting an assault on the house, so place 12 **assault_rally** points down behind the cover. Name them Gather_here01 - Gather_here12.

Like all other entities, there are certain properties associated with rally points, which can drastically change how they function. The most important ones are:

- The **name** property
- The **assault point** property
- The **assault delay** property
- The **urgent** property

The **assault point** specifies the assault point we want our NPC to eventually go to. The **assault delay** specifies a time, in seconds, to wait before assaulting. The **urgent** property will force the NPC to move to this point, ignoring his/her surroundings. Set the **assault point** property to **assault_here**, set the **assault delay** to **3**, and set the **urgent** property to **yes**. Copy those properties to the other rally points.

Placing assault goals

The last entity we need to make this assault work is the **ai_goal_assault** entity. This entity will kick the whole assault into motion. By default, this entity is disabled. Once activated, each NPC involved in the assault will move to its rally point and wait for the signal to begin the assault. Once that signal is received, the NPC will wait the specified amount of time and then begin the assault.

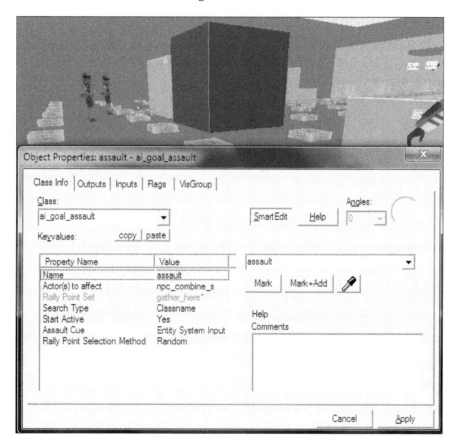

Place an **ai_goal_assault** entity anywhere in your map. Name it `assault` and change the properties, detailed in the following sections:

Actors to affect

Set **actors to affect** to **npc_combine_s**. When used in conjunction with **search type** set to **classname**, this will involve all of the combine soldiers in the map in the assault. You can also search for a specific entity name as well. If you wanted a soldier named Richard to assault a different area, you would set **search type** to **entity name** and the **actors to affect** field to `Richard`.

Setting rally points

The **rally point set** property tells the NPCs where to position themselves before they get the assault command. Typing `gather_here*` will set all rally points that start with **gather_here** to be proper rally points.

 You could also have each rally point have the same name, and only put one entity name in for the **rally point set** parameter.

Search type

Change **search type** to look for either entity names or entity class types. In our case, we want to search for a specific class. The class we're searching for is specified in the **actors to affect** property, which we have already set to **npc_combine_s**.

Start active

If **start active** is set to **yes**, the NPCs involved will move to their rally points as soon as the map is loaded. If this is set to **no**, we would have to fire an **activate** input to move the NPCs into position. In this case, set this to **yes**.

Rally Point Selection Method

Each rally point can have a priority with the lowest number being the most important. Since we have 12 rally points and 12 NPCs, it really doesn't matter which point has the highest priority because every rally point will be filled. Change this to **random** so that each NPC will pick whichever rally point they want. When everything is set up, place a button on the inside wall of the house that will begin the assault:

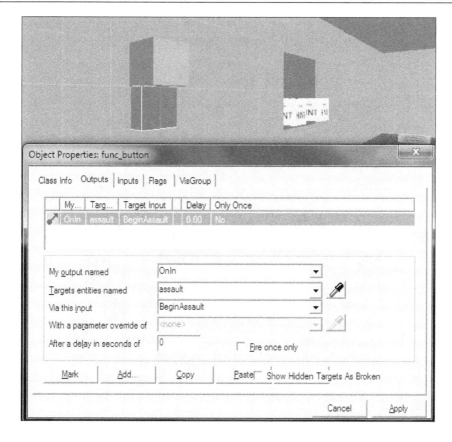

You need to create the following output:

```
OnIn > assault > beginassault > 0.00s delay
```

Compile and play the map to see the results!

During combat, the soldiers will assault the house, moving towards the assault point whenever they can, as shown in the following image:

Creating squads

You'll probably notice that the NPCs fend for themselves. There's no communication, there's no guarding one another, they run as individuals, and they die alone. **Squads** can be used to change battle behavior and amplify the effect of a group in combat.

Your first squad

The only way to create a squad is to give a group of NPCs the same squad name. In fact, that's really all the work you have to do! NPCs within the same squad will call out enemies, cover each other, inform squad mates of enemy locations, and call for help when they need it. So long as you have a decent array of navigation and hint nodes, simply assigning NPCs to a squad is all the work needed to increase their effectiveness in the battle.

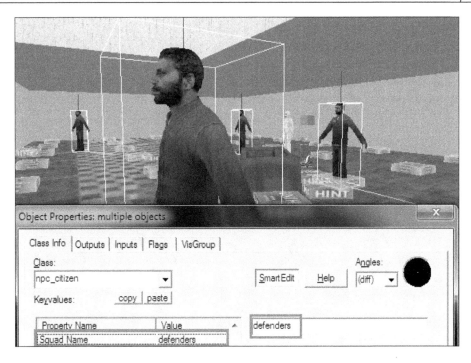

Scripting a flank

Using some entities we've learned about already, we can script a **flank** on the citizens inside the house. Select six of the combine soldiers and assign them the names `alpha_soldier01-alpha_soldier06`. Put them in a **squad** called **alpha**. We will be using a **math_counter** entity to initiate the flank. When three members of the **alpha squad** are killed, the other three will run around the side of the house to try to flank the citizens. We'll be using an **aiscripted_schedule** entity that tells the remaining members of the alpha squad to initiate the flanking maneuvre.

Creating a schedule and a path

Place an **aiscripted_schedule** entity near the side entrance of the house, along with a path of about 4 to 5 **path_corners** leading from the front corner, around the house, and inside the house. Name the **path_corners** `alpha_flank01-alpha_flank05`. You already have some experience with **aiscripted schedules**, but we're going to override the AI and force them to complete this schedule in the middle of a battle.

Aiscripted schedules

Here is how you can set up this schedule:

```
Name: alpha_start_flank
Target NPC: alpha_soldier*
All in Radius: Yes
Schedule to run: Run Goal Path
Interruptability: Death
Goal Entity: alpha_path01
```

Remember that an asterisk after a name will find all entities matching the base name. Setting the **target NPC** entity to **alpha_soldier*** will find **alpha_soldier01-06**. When you see **All in radius = yes**, this means it will find all matching NPCs instead of stopping the moment any one is found. **Schedule to run** is self-explanatory; run along the goal path. **Interruptability** set to **death** means so long as the NPC is alive, it will complete the script—nothing can stop the soldiers except a few well-placed bullets. **Goal entity** is the start of our path; in this case, **alpha_path01**. The soldiers will automatically follow the other **path_corners** entity until the end and resume their normal AI behavior once there.

Aiscripted schedule flags

There are a few flags we want to set as well that are mentioned as follows:

```
Repeatable: No
Search Cyclically: Yes
Don't Complain: Yes
```

We only want this script to run once, so there's no reason for it to be **repeatable**. **Search cyclically** will ensure that each NPC found will run the schedule. **Don't complain** will prevent any navigation errors from being displayed on the console.

Math counter

The **math counter** entity will trigger an output when its internal counter reaches a certain value. For us, we want it to trigger an output when the counter reaches 3. Place a **math_counter** entity and check out the properties, as shown in the following image:

Let's examine some of the **math_counter** properties:

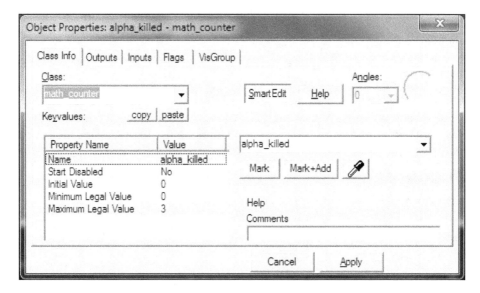

An output can trigger when the counter value reaches either **minimum** or **maximum legal value**. In our case, we want to fire an output when **Maximum Legal Value** reaches **3**. The output will look like this:

```
OnHitMax > alpha_start_flank > StartSchedule > 0.00ms Delay
```

Setting up our soldiers

The **math_counter** property needs inputs before it can start counting. The soldiers (**npc_combine_s**) have outputs that are triggered to death. So, when a soldier in **alpha squad** is killed, we want to increase our **math_counter** by 1.

```
OnDeath > alpha_killed > add > 1 > 0.00s Delay
```

Any input over **3** will have no effect.

That's it, we're all set up. You'll see the soldiers run to flank the citizens inside the house once enough of them have gotten shot down. The citizens, although fewer in number, are pretty well-guarded and will probably win the fight. Try changing the soldier weapon types, aggression (the **Tactical variant** property), and grenade count to sway the battle outcome.

Summary

Info node entities are a necessary addition to any map containing NPC combat. They guide the NPC movements, and hint nodes can control special NPC behaviors at certain points. Controlling groups of NPCs is easy with assaults, and creating squads can further increase the effectiveness of a group combat.

11
Source Particle Editor

One of the many great things offered in the Source authoring tools is Particle Editor. Waterfalls, fire effects, weapon effects, explosions, and more can all be created with particles. A particle system is a group of particles—2D sprites—with different rules applied to them. You can apply forces, transparency, and even parent particles to other entities.

In this chapter you will learn the following:

- Booting HL2 into tools mode
- Creating particle systems
- Importing particle systems into maps
- Creating the particle manifest file
- Having some fun with fireworks

The particle effects are created and edited within the game *HalfLife 2: Episode Two*, but you first need to gain access to the tools menu. Let's get started!

Accessing the tools menu

The tools menu needs to be enabled with a special launch option, -tools. It may also benefit you to run the game with the -novid option so the Valve intro movie does not play. To set launch options, open the Steam **Library**, right-click on your Source game and select **Properties**. In the **GENERAL** tab, click on **SET LAUNCH OPTIONS...** and enter -novid -console -tools, as shown in the following screenshot.

This will cause the game to quickly boot into tools mode and you can then load the console.

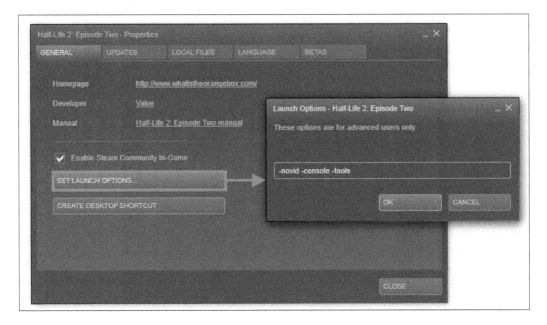

Using Particle Editor

When you load the game you won't see the standard splash screen or background screen. Instead, you'll be greeted by a 3D window and a toolbar. Under the **Tools** tab, select **Particle Editor** to load Particle Editor tools:

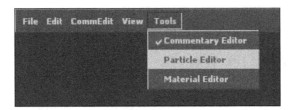

Create a new particle system by clicking on **File | New**. You will see the view has now changed dramatically.

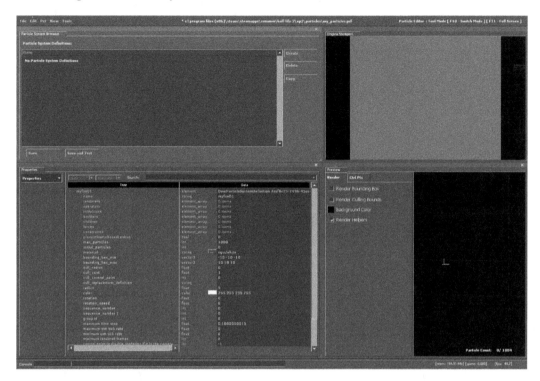

Welcome to Particle Editor! The top-left window lists all the particles within `*.pcffile` (the file that contains the particle scripts) and it also lets you create, copy, and delete particle systems. The top-right window is an engine preview. If you don't have a map loaded, you will not see anything. Press the *F10* key to switch to the engine view, and then press *F11* to make it full screen. You can now load any map you want. At any time, you can press *F11* to minimize the window and then press *F10* to go back into tools mode. The bottom-left window is where we'll be spending most of our time; it's where all the particle properties are set and tweaked. The bottom-right window will display a preview of the particle effect you're working on. Left-clicking in the preview window will rotate the view, while right-clicking will zoom in and out. Holding *Shift* and left-clicking will pan the view.

There are many options available to you in Particle Editor, but we'll get to see how each one works in the examples to come. Innumerable particle effects can be created with Particle Editor, but the first step towards the path of enlightenment starts with fire.

Creating a fire particle

Click on **Create** and name the particle system myfire01. This is the name that Hammer will reference when compiling a map.

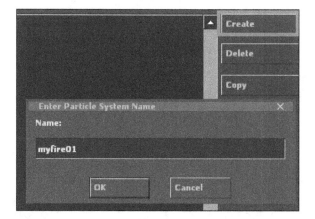

Before we continue, let's save the system. Name it my_particles and place it in the SteamApps\common\Mod\particles folder. For EP2, it would go here: SteamApps\common\Half-Life 2\ep2\particles. The *.pcf file we just saved contains multiple different types of particles. Again, when referenced, Hammer will look for the particle system name, not the PCF filename, so keep this in mind while naming any future particles.

The first thing you will see upon creation of the particle is the **Properties** list. The default material applied to any new particle is vgui/white with a render color of white and a radius of five units. Let's leave this as default for now because it's much easier to simply get something rendered before we start tweaking our settings.

Creating particles

It's helpful to have an idea of what you want to create before you start. If you imagine how fire acts, the flames begin within a small area, rise up, and then fade out. New flames constantly take the place of the old ones. With this in mind, we can work on the initial creation of the particles.

Using Emitter

In the **Properties** dropdown, select **Emitter** as shown in the following screenshot:

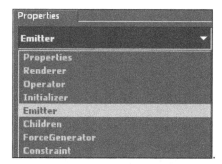

The **Emitter** tab controls how your particles are created or emitted. The two main options here are **emit_continuously** and **emit_instantaneously**. As you have probably guessed, **emit_continuously** will constantly emit particles and **emit_instantaneously** will emit a lot of particles all at once. Since we're making fire and fire constantly creates new flames, we want to use **emit_continuously**. Right-click in the blank list beneath the drop-down list and select **Add... | emit_continuously**.

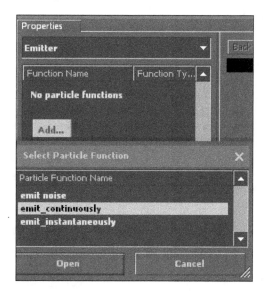

We can now see the data list that is attributed to the **emit_continuously** property. Our main concern right now is the emission rate, which is quantified in particles per second. The default value is 100, which will mean an emission rate of 100 particles per second. Our future changes will be easier to see if we slow this down to about 20, so change **emission_rate** to 20 to spawn 20 particles per second.

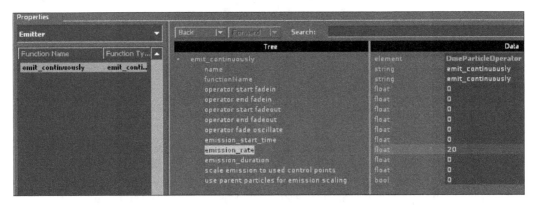

We can't see anything in the particle preview yet, but we're only on step one.

Using Renderer

The next step is to select how we want our particles rendered. The default fire sprites have the ability to animate themselves. Therefore, we will select **render_animated_sprites**. This can also be used for particles without animations and is usually the default particle renderer.

Now that we have told the particle system how to display the sprite, we can see a preview! It's nothing special right now, just a white box, but it's a start! This white box is actually a collection of hundreds of sprites all rendered on top of one another. There's a default maximum particle amount of 1000, so older particles will be culled when the count reaches 1000. Fire doesn't start from a single point; it's usually spread across an area, so let's make that happen.

Using Initializer

Each particle that is created has a multitude of different properties associated with it. Some examples of these properties are: alpha (transparency), lifetime, speed, and color. Each of these properties can be modified during or after particle creation. The properties that are set during creation are called initializers. Let's spread out the fire particles' origin to a set area. We can randomize the initial position of each particle within a certain area by adding the **Position Within Box Random** property under the **Initializer** tab:

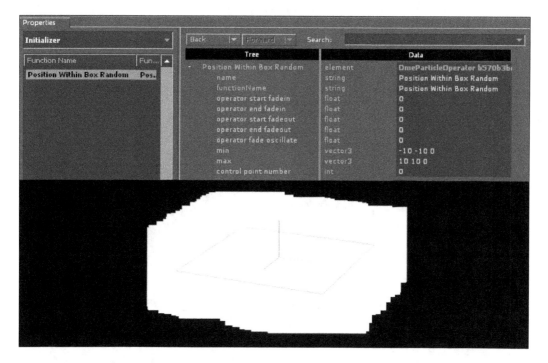

The two properties we want to change here are the **min** and **max** values. They hold values in an X Y Z format and by default are set to 0 0 0. Set **min** to -10 -10 0 and **max** to 10 10 0 to have the particles spawn within a 20 x 20 box centered about the origin. You can see the bounds of the spawn area depicted by a yellow outline and you will also see the particles randomly spawn within that area.

The next logical step is to give our particles some initial velocity so we can simulate the rise of the flames. Let's create a **Velocity Random** initializer so we can give some life to our white box flames. Again, we're dealing with random values, so we have to set minimum and maximum values. The values are named: **speed_in_local_coordinate_system_min** and **speed_in_local_coordinate_system_max**. Set them to 0 0 30 and 0 0 90 respectively; this will set a random vertical speed between 30 to 90 for each particle. The properties have long names but they do describe their functions clearly. As an example, if you rotate the particle system in Hammer by 45 degrees, the flames will travel at a 45 degree angle. The local direction of the particles is still set to a positive Z direction (straight up), but since the particle system itself has been rotated, the direction will change.

Operator

The properties in the operator give us control over the particles after they've been created. We gave our particles a random initial velocity but they're not moving yet. We need to actually enable movement in the operator group before the particles will move. In the operator tab, add a **movement basic** property. Once that's done, you will see the white boxes rise up.

Awesome! We have hundreds of little white boxes rising into the air. Now is a great time to choose our fire material. In the main drop-down menu, go to the **Properties** tab and find the **material** property. Click on the box with the ellipsis (**...**) to open the material browser.

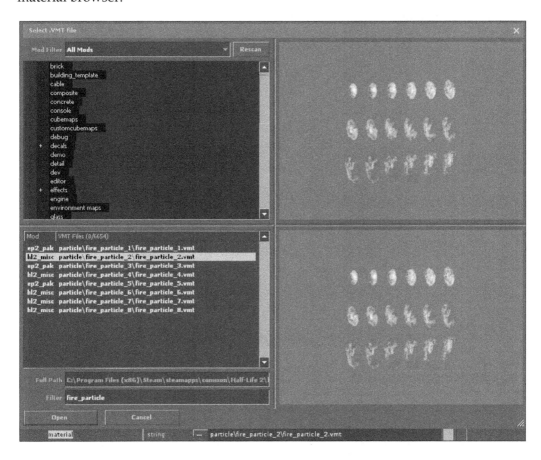

Filter for `fire_particle` and `fire_particle_2` and click on **Open**. You should now see an orange puff of fire replace the white boxes in the preview window. The fire doesn't seem animated because the default animation rate is quite low. Go into the **Renderer** tab and change **animation rate** to 1. Your fire sprites are now animated as they rise up—neat!

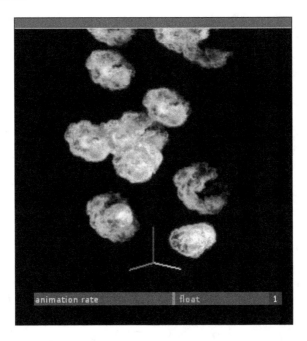

Our particle system is starting to take shape, but our effect isn't really convincing as our particles are rather thin now. We need to give it some more volume. It's hard to gauge the scale of the effect without anything else in the preview window, but remember that the default radius is five units and our particles are spawning in a 20 x 20 box. We can beef up the flames a bit with an initialization property called **radius random**. You can experiment with the **radius_max** and **radius_min** values to get the effect you want, but I've found that the effect produced by a minimum radius of 10 and a maximum radius of 30 looks quite nice.

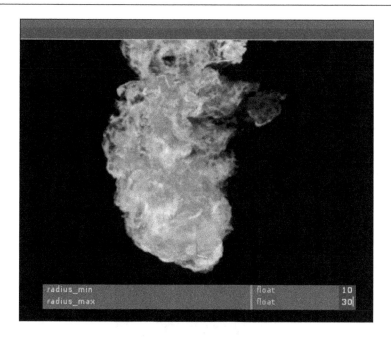

Hey, it's actually starting to look like a fire! Note two things: the flames rise forever and never fade out, and all the fire particles are facing the same direction. This kills some of the realism but it's easily fixed with a few more properties.

In real life, flames have both a random transparency and a random lifetime. We have options for both of these in the **Initializer** group. Add a **lifetime_random** property with a minimum value of 0.5 (seconds) and a maximum value of 1. If you haven't guessed already, this will randomize the lifetime of each particle between the minimum and maximum values. However, the addition of the property won't do anything until we add in a **lifespan decay operator** property.

We have the flames lasting for random amounts of time, but to add another ounce of realism, we should be able to see through the fire. Remember, the alpha of an entity, (particle in this case) is the **transparency** ranging from 0 to 255. An **alpha** value of 0 is fully transparent and a value of 255 will render an entirely opaque entity. Add an alpha random initializer with a minimum value of 10 and a maximum value of 180. We can also make the flames fade out before they finally disappear. The **alpha fade** and **decay operator** properties will lower the alpha based off the time the particle exits. If we start the fadeout at 0.5 and end it at 1, the particle will begin fading out when half of its life has passed. It will be fully transparent when it is removed from the particle system.

There's one final property we can add to this fire to finish the effect. Add a **rotation random** initializer, keeping the default values to give the particles a random rotation upon spawning. In the end, we have a very neat-looking fire effect. Let's put it inside a level!

Particles manifest

In order for us to put the particles in a level, we need to create what is called a `particles_manifest.txt` file. The particles manifest tells the engine where to locate our particle systems and when to load them into a map. You need to create one manifest file for each map in which you have particles in addition to the master.

Master manifest

The master particles manifest file needs to contain all the custom `.pcf` files you have created with Particle Editor. Browse to your mod's `particles` folder and create a new `.txt` file called `particles_manifest.txt`. Type the following and then save the file:

```
particles_manifest
{
    file   "particles/my_particles.pcf"
}
```

I have included a sample `particles_manifest.txt` file along with the `my_particles.pcf` file so that you can refer to them.

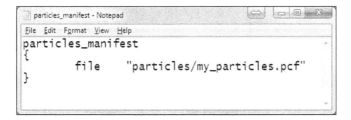

The map-specific manifest

As previously noted, each map needs its own manifest file in order to load the correct particles. The per-map manifest goes into the `maps` folder and contains the map name `*_particles`. In my example, `mapch12_example.bsp` will need a manifest file titled `ch12_example_particles.txt`. It follows the same format as the master manifest file located in the `particles` folder but you only need to include the `.pcf` files that will be used in that map.

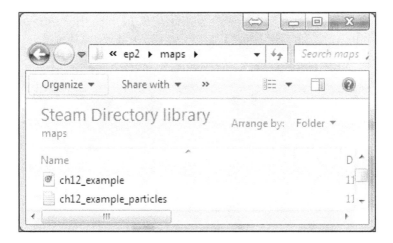

The info particle system

Let's insert our new fire particle into Hammer. If our `particles_manifest.txt` file is coded properly and is in the correct locations, all we need to do is place an entity and reference the file. Then, create or load a map and place the point entity `info_particle_system`.

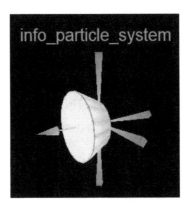

Open the properties for `info_particle_system` and type `myfire01` in the **Particle System Name** field. This is not the name of the `.pcf` file; it's the name of the particle system within the `.pcf` file! Set **Start Active?** to **yes** and we're done!

Compile and load the map to check our results in game.

Particle systems cannot emit light! In the preceding example, I used a separate orange light entity to simulate the fire's light output.

Particle children

Particle systems, just like other entities, can have parent-child relationships. The entity `info_particle_system` can be parented to any entity, but particle systems within a `.pcf` file can also be parented to each other. To demonstrate this, let's create a quick smoke effect to add to the fire.

Modifying existing particle systems

Instead of creating a whole other smoke effect from scratch, we can just copy and modify the fire particle. In Particle Editor, select the particle system **myfire01**, and click on the **Copy** button. Type `mysmoke01` for the new particle name and click on **OK**.

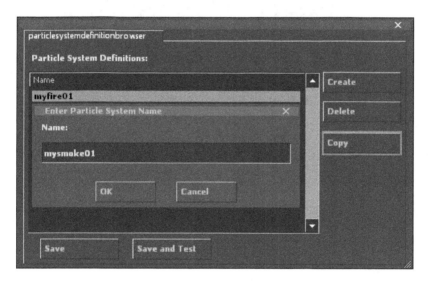

Now we have an exact copy of our fire particle system with a new name. Select the new particle system and let's turn it into a smoke system.

The first thing we want to change is the material. In the main properties, browse for the material **particle | smoke1 | smoke1_additive.vmt**. You'll see the fire change to smoke. But we're not done quite yet. When there is a fire, smoke doesn't appear immediately; it forms gradually and fades out slowly. Let's recreate that.

In the operator tab, remove the **alpha fade** and **decay operator** properties, and add **alpha fade in random** and **alpha fade out random**. Set both the minimum values to 0.2, and set the maximum values to 0.5. Leave the rest of the settings at default. You should see the smoke fade in and out.

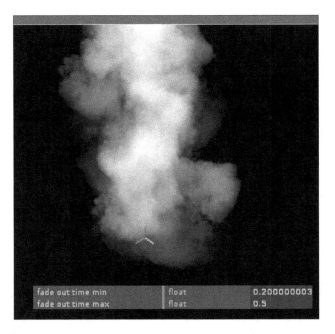

We also know that smoke has the tendency to expand as it fades out. We can add a property that will dynamically change the radius of the particle. Add a **radius scale** property in the **Operator** tab, and change the following properties:

- **Start_time**: 0.5
- **End_time**: 1
- **Radius_start_scale**: 1
- **Radius_end_scale**: 2
- **Scale_bias**: 0

The very last thing to do to our smoke sprite is to change the lifetime. The smoke will linger longer than the flames. So in the **lifetime_random** initializer, change **lifetime_min** to 2.75 and **lifetime_max** to 3. We now have a pretty good-looking smoke effect. Let's combine it with the fire.

Create a new particle system called `myfire_and_smoke01`. In the **Children** tab, add **myfire01** and **mysmoke01** to the list—that's it! You're done. Check the preview tab to see both your particle effects overlaid in a pretty convincing smoky fire.

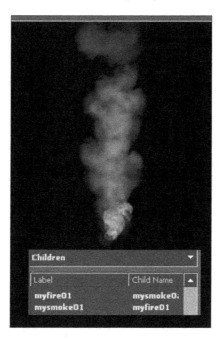

Making fireworks

We can make a firework effect just as easily as fire and smoke. Let's first think about how fireworks act. They fly into the air and instantly explode into hundreds of balls of light. Gravity takes over after the initial explosion, and as the balls of light fall back to earth, they fade out. We're going to make our particle system create hundreds of particles instantly, have those particles fly out from the center, be affected by gravity, and fade out. As for the flying into the air part, we will parent the particle system to a `func_physbox` entity and launch it into the air.

In Particle Editor, create a new particle system called `firework01`.

Creating the explosion

When creating particles, it's good practice to start with an emitter like we have done with the fire effect. Unlike the fire, however, we're going to use an **emit_ instantaneously** property to create a bunch of particles at the same time. Change the **num_to_emit** value to 250 to create 250 particles instantaneously.

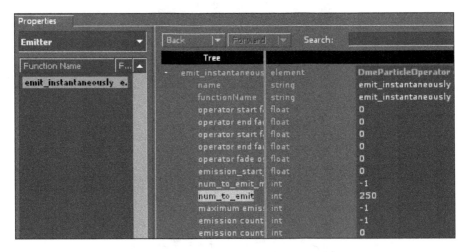

Just like before, the next step is to set up the renderer. Add a render_animated_ sprites renderer and we can see that we have the familiar white square in our preview window. Also note that the particle count is 250/1004.

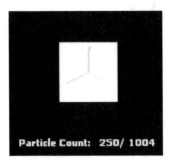

We haven't set up a decay yet, so everything is looking good so far with 250 live particles.

The next step is creating the explosion. We'll need an initializer property to create the initial movement, so in the **Initializer** tab, add a **Velocity Random** property. Set **speed_in_local_coordinate_system_min** to -250 -250 -250 and **speed_in_local_ coordinate_system_max** to 250 250 250. This will create a random velocity between 0 and 250 units per second in every direction.

Our 3D preview isn't showing anything yet, because we still need a **movement_basic** operator to enable motion. Add one in to watch your little white boxes fly away.

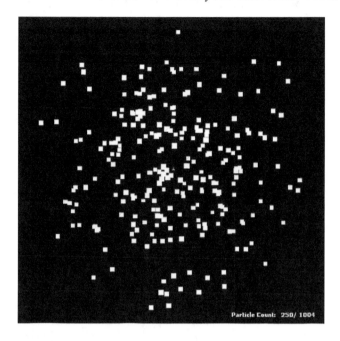

Simulating gravity

We know that the pieces of fireworks fall because of gravity, so let's simulate that effect. While you still have the **movement_basic** property open, change **gravity** to 0 0 -100 and give the system a **drag** value of 0.05 to slow everything down. You should see the particles fire out from the center, slow to a crawl, and be pulled back down due to gravity.

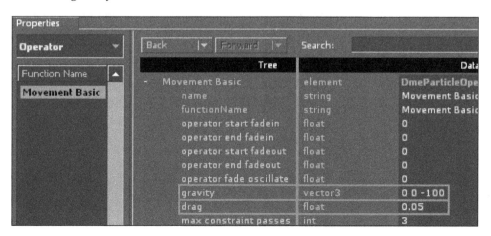

Fading and other properties

While we're in the **Operator** tab, add in the alpha fade and decay properties. Leave everything to its default value, but set **start_fade_out_time** to 0.5 so that the particles begin fading out when they've lived 50 percent of their lives.

At this point, you will see the particles fade out predictably, but real fireworks don't do that; the sparks die out randomly. Add a lifetime random property in the **Initializer** tab and set the **lifetime_min** and **lifetime_max** fields to 1 and 2 respectively. Now it looks like we have the basics of a decent firework. Note the different alpha values of the particles.

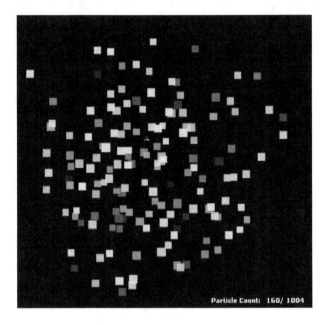

Fireworks don't look like white boxes, so let's change the white box into a nice glow sprite and give the effect a burst of color. While we're still in the **Initializer** tab, add a color random property and pick two colors of your choice for **color1** and **color2**. Each spawned particle will have a color somewhere between the two colors. Also add a Position Within a Sphere Random property with a **radius_max** value of 2. If this isn't done, the particle will always be created at the map's origin!

In the **Properties** tab of the particle effect, assign **particle | particle_glow_10.vmt** in the material field to get rid of that unsightly square.

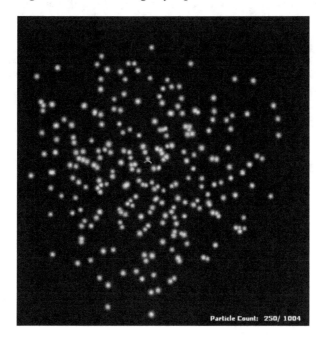

Since we've already created a manifest file, we can call our firework particle complete.

A parenting example

We're going to create a firework entity set up using Hammer that will launch a Shell into the air, explode, and display our firework effect. We'll need the following entities:

- **Func_physbox**
- **Phys_thruster**
- **Phys_keepupright**
- **Info_particle_system**
- **Ambient_generic x 2**

And, of course, we'll need **func_button** to set everything in motion.

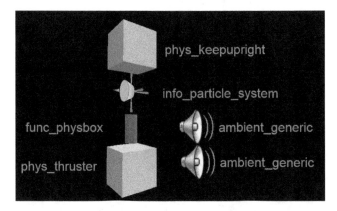

Here's how it's going to work: the **func_physbox** entity will act as our firework Shell. It will be thrust into the air by a **phys_thruster** entity. Since we want a controlled ascent, we will use **phys_keepupright** to keep the Shell pointed straight up. The **info_particle_system** will display the firework effect in air, and the sounds will give us the launch and explosion ambience. Let's get to work!

Setting up the shell

The Shell is a **func_physbox** which is a brush entity. Create an eight-sided cylinder that has the dimensions 6 x 6 x 6 units. Tie it to a **func_physbox** entity and name it Shell. Nothing else needs to be done for the **func_physbox** entity.

Launching the shell

Create a **phys_thruster** point entity below the Shell and set the following properties:

- **Name**: Shell_Thruster
- **Attached Object**: Shell
- **Time of Force**: 2
- **Force**: 1000

Set **angles** to **Up** and make sure you check the **Ignore Mass** flag. The **phys_thruster** will apply an upwards force on the Shell for two seconds, thus launching it into the air.

Stabilizing the shell

Since the **phys_thruster** entity can be a bit unpredictable at times, we should stabilize the shell with **phys_keepupright**. Place one in the map near the shell and give it the following properties:

- **Target Entity**: Shell
- **Angular Limit**: 60

The **Target Entity** is the affected physics object; in our case, that would be the Shell. The **Angular Limit** specifies the maximum number of degrees per second that the **phys_keepupright** can correct the orientation of the shell by. We don't need to change the value of **Angles** for the **phys_keepupright** entity, because we never changed this for the shell. Since a value of 0 0 0 is considered to be upright, the **phys_keepupright** entity will try to maintain these angles.

 Sixty degrees per second is a very safe **Angular Limit** value; this guarantees that our shell will stay vertical. Try experimenting with lower values to give your shell an unexpected wobble on the way up.

Setting up the particle

Place an **info_particle_system** entity on top of the shell.

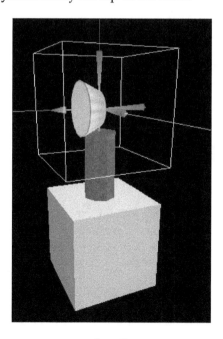

Give it the following properties:

- **Name**: Shell_particle
- **Parent**: Shell
- **Particle System Name**: firework01
- **Start Active**: No

Since we've parented the particle system to the shell, wherever the shell goes, the particle system goes.

Adding sound effects

What's the fun of fireworks if they don't make any noise? Place two **ambient_generic** entities so we can emulate the launch and explosion sounds of a firework. Set the following properties for the first one:

- **Name**: Shell_thrust_sound
- **Sound Name**: rocketfire1.wav
- **SourceEntityName**: Shell

This first **ambient_generic** entity is the sound we want to use when the shell is first launched; it's the same sound the Rocket Launcher weapon makes in *Half-Life 2*. The **SourceEntityName** will cause a sound to be emitted from the shell, making it more convincing.

The second **ambient_generic** entity should be set up as follows:

- **Name**: Shell_explode_sound
- **Sound Name**: explode4.wav
- **SourceEntityName**: Shell

Tying everything together

In your **func_button** entity, add the following outputs:

```
OnIn, Shell_Thruster, Activate, 0.00s Delay
OnIn, Shell_Thrust_sound, PlaySound, 0.00s Delay
OnIn, Shell_Particle, Start, 2.50s Delay
OnIn, Shell_explode_sound, PlaySound, 2.50s Delay
OnIn, Shell_particle, ClearParent, 2.50s Delay
OnIn, Shell, Kill, 2.51s Delay
OnIn, Shell_Particle, Stop, 5.51s Delay
```

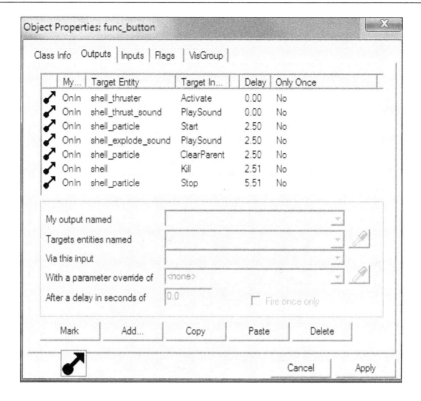

The first two outputs activate the thruster and the sound effect as soon as the button is pushed. The third and fourth outputs will display the firework effect and play the sound. The fifth output clears the parent of the particle system, and the sixth output destroys the shell.

We clear the particle system's parent before killing the shell because if the parent dies, all its children die as well. If we didn't do this, the particle system would not display properly because its parent would be dead. The last output stops the particle effect after its maximum possible duration of three seconds.

Results

The following is what the setup looks like:

The following is what the launch looks like:

And the finale is shown as follows:

We could have spent a few more minutes adding more fire effects to the rocket, tweaking the timings, and perfecting the particle systems, but this is a good start.

Summary

Particles are a worthy addition to any map or mod. Particle Editor has a pretty tough to pick up, but I hope that with this chapter as a foundation, and some extra time spent using the editor, you will perfect it. Particles can be used for fire, fireworks, waterfalls, or any other effect you can dream of. Their ability to be parented to other entities can greatly increase the visual effects of any entity set up.

I want to thank you for reading this book. Creating maps for *Half-Life 1* and *Half-Life 2* has been my passion for over a decade. It gives me great pleasure to share my knowledge and experience with you. By now, you should have the tools you need to unleash your imagination within the Source engine. Get out there and start creating! Good luck and goodbye.

Index

operator **246-250**
outputs, trigger once entity
  adding 163, 164
overlays
  about 26
  applying 90

P

Paint Alpha tool
  used, for creating displacement 98, 99
Paint Geometry tool
  used, for creating displacement 94-96
panning camera 187, 188
particle children 253
Particle Editor
  about 239
  fire particle, creating 242
  particles, creating 242
  using 240, 241
particles
  about 239
  creating 242
  creating, Emitter used 243, 244
  creating, Initializer used 245, 246
  creating, Renderer used 244, 245
  creating, with operator 246-250
  particle children 253
particles manifest
  about 250
  info particle system 252
  map-specific manifest 251
  master manifest 250, 251
path 177
Path_track 178
physics props
  creating 108, 109
Pitch property 70
player-controlled track trains
  about 177, 178
  controlling 181
  func_tracktrain entity, creating 178
  Func_traincontrols 178
  path, creating 179, 180
  Path_track 178
  tying, to path 180, 181

point camera
  about 184-186
  multiple camera 187
  panning camera 187, 188
pointfile entity 153
point lights
  using 124-127
point light source
  placing 137-139
point viewcontrol
  about 188
  camera 189, 190
  camera path 191, 192
projected textures
  using 135-137
props
  creating 106
  dynamic props, creating 109
  physics props, creating 108, 109
  static props, creating 106-108

R

RAD 148, 149
Raise To option
  used, for creating displacement 97
rally points
  placing 228
Ray-Traced Preview 24
Renderer
  using 244, 245

S

Scaling mode 43, 46
schedule
  triggering 206
schedule, flank
  aiscripted schedule flags 235
  aiscripted schedules 234
scripted sequences
  about 206, 207
  animation, selecting 207, 208
  combining 209, 211
sculpting tool
  using 102-104

Thank you for buying
Source SDK Game Development Essentials

About Packt Publishing

Packt, pronounced 'packed', published its first book *"Mastering phpMyAdmin for Effective MySQL Management"* in April 2004 and subsequently continued to specialize in publishing highly focused books on specific technologies and solutions.

Our books and publications share the experiences of your fellow IT professionals in adapting and customizing today's systems, applications, and frameworks. Our solution based books give you the knowledge and power to customize the software and technologies you're using to get the job done. Packt books are more specific and less general than the IT books you have seen in the past. Our unique business model allows us to bring you more focused information, giving you more of what you need to know, and less of what you don't.

Packt is a modern, yet unique publishing company, which focuses on producing quality, cutting-edge books for communities of developers, administrators, and newbies alike. For more information, please visit our website: www.packtpub.com.

Writing for Packt

We welcome all inquiries from people who are interested in authoring. Book proposals should be sent to author@packtpub.com. If your book idea is still at an early stage and you would like to discuss it first before writing a formal book proposal, contact us; one of our commissioning editors will get in touch with you.

We're not just looking for published authors; if you have strong technical skills but no writing experience, our experienced editors can help you develop a writing career, or simply get some additional reward for your expertise.

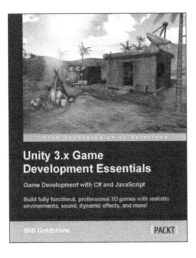

Unity 3.x Game Development Essentials

ISBN: 978-1-84969-144-4   Paperback: 488 pages

Build fully functional, professional 3D games with realistic environments, sound, dynamic effects, and more!

1. Kick start your game development, and build ready-to-play 3D games with ease.

2. Understand key concepts in game design including scripting, physics, instantiation, particle effects, and more.

3. Test and optimize your game to perfection with essential tips and tricks.

Unity 3D Game Development by Example Beginner's Guide

ISBN: 978-1-84969-054-6   Paperback: 384 pages

A seat-of-your-pants manual for building fun, groovy little games quickly

1. Build fun games using the free Unity 3D game engine even if you've never coded before.

2. Learn how to "skin" projects to make totally different games from the same file – more games, less effort!

3. Deploy your games to the Internet so that your friends and family can play them.

4. Packed with ideas, inspiration, and advice for your own game design and development.

Please check **www.PacktPub.com** for information on our titles

XNA 4.0 Game Development by Example Beginner's Guide

ISBN: 978-1-84969-066-9   Paperback: 428 pages

Create exciting games with Microsoft XNA 4.0

1. Dive headfirst into game creation with XNA.

2. Four different styles of games comprising a puzzler, a space shooter, a multi-axis shoot 'em up, and a jump-and-run platformer.

3. Games that gradually increase in complexity to cover a wide variety of game development techniques.

4. Focuses entirely on developing games with the free version of XNA.

Starling Game Development Essentials

ISBN: 978-1-78398-354-4   Paperback: 116 pages

Develop and deploy isometric turn-based games using Starling

1. Create a cross-platform Starling Isometric game.

2. Add enemy AI and multiplayer capability.

3. Explore the complete source code for the Web and cross-platform game develpment.

Please check **www.PacktPub.com** for information on our titles